"If life improves, there is hope."

Several thought leaders share their views in this commemorative monograph to inspire the younger generation to better the lives of people. If we fail, we can become a mercenary society, and this is not what we want our future Singapore to be.

Valuable ideas on effective parenting and suggestions to create different pathways to success are presented. The young need to acquire skills in managing the digital world, to close the social divide and to fight human exploitation.

Dr S Vasoo
Emeritus Professor, Department of Social Work,
Faculty of Arts & Social Sciences
National University of Singapore

A wonderful compilation of thought-provoking lectures captured over the past seven years — questions are re-casted and answered with a current-day lens. This publication provides much needed discourse on systemic issues affecting children and youth in Singapore. A highly recommended read!

Ms Anita Fam
President, National Council of Social Service

I congratulate the Singapore Children's Society on its 70th anniversary. The children of Singapore are fortunate to have you as their champion.

Every year, the Children's Society invites an expert or a leader to deliver its lecture. This book contains six lectures delivered between 2015 and 2021. Han Fook Kwang talks about the digital revolution and its many benefits. However, the internet also threatens children with online bullying and other issues. Teo You

Yenn tells us that children from lower-income families face low self-esteem, poor home environments and are unable to compete with children from higher-income families. The wonderful John Elliott, who died too soon, says that there is no single model of good parenting. What's important is for the parents to be sincerely concerned about their children's welfare. And I agree with Priscilla Lui that corporal punishment of children should be banned. This book also contains two thoughtful lectures by Minister Grace Fu and Minister Chan Chun Sing. I am happy to recommend this book to anyone who is interested in children.

Professor Tommy Koh
Ambassador-at-Large, Ministry of Foreign Affairs

Thinking of
Children

The Singapore Children's Society
Collected Lectures (2015 – 2021)

Recommended Titles

Speaking of Children: The Singapore Children's Society Collected Lectures
by Singapore Children's Society
ISBN: 978-981-4699-27-3

Thinking of

Children

The Singapore Children's Society
Collected Lectures (2015 – 2021)

Children's
SOCIETY
Caring for the Future
——— Since 1952 ———

70 years
of bringing hope
and smiles

World Scientific

Published by

World Scientific Publishing Co. Pte. Ltd.

5 Toh Tuck Link, Singapore 596224

USA office: 27 Warren Street, Suite 401-402, Hackensack, NJ 07601

UK office: 57 Shelton Street, Covent Garden, London WC2H 9HE

National Library Board, Singapore Cataloguing in Publication Data

Name(s): Singapore Children's Society.

Title: Thinking of children : the Singapore Children's Society collected lectures (2015–2021).

Description: Singapore : World Scientific Publishing Co. Pte. Ltd., [2022]

Identifier(s): ISBN 978-981-12-6131-2 | 978-981-12-6080-3 (paperback) |
    978-981-12-6081-0 (ebook for institutions) | 978-981-12-6082-7 (ebook for individuals)

Subject(s): LCSH: Children--Services for--Singapore. | Child welfare--Singapore.

Classification: DDC 362.7095957--dc23

British Library Cataloguing-in-Publication Data

A catalogue record for this book is available from the British Library.

With Support From:

SINGAPORE

S

*For Community
Purpose and Benefit*

P O O L S

For any available supplementary material, please visit
https://www.worldscientific.com/worldscibooks/10.1142/12983#t=suppl

Desk Editor: Nicole Ong

Typeset by Stallion Press
Email: enquiries@stallionpress.com

This book is dedicated to the children and youths of Singapore and to the late Dr John M. Elliott who was Chair of the Book Committee for the first book in this series, *Speaking of Children: The Singapore Children's Society Collected Lectures.*

Singapore Children's Society's commitment to raising public awareness on issues pertinent to the well-being of children, youth and families resonates strongly with Singapore Pools' vision of building an inclusive and caring Singapore.

We are proud to partner Singapore Children's Society in making the second book in its series of collected lectures available to a wider audience.

With support from:

SINGAPORE

POOLS

**For Community
Purpose and Benefit**

Foreword

Childhood in Singapore has seen dramatic changes over the decades. In the realms of education, healthcare, social services and legislation, there have been advancements made to enable as many children as possible to reach their fullest potential. Our children have also been able to harness the benefits of technology and new media for enhanced learning that extends beyond the confines of classroom walls.

Even so, there are challenges, both emergent and constant, that children and their families face. The advent of the digital world has brought about issues relating to online safety. Lower-income families, while endeavouring for better livelihoods, further navigate a host of complex obstacles in pulling their children out from the poverty gap. Beyond basic needs, we are also cognisant of children's social-emotional needs of growing up in a safe, secure and nurturing environment.

What are the systemic issues that affect the everyday, lived realities of the children in Singapore? And how do we remain nimble and creative in finding solutions for them? As we recover from the compounding impact of the Covid-19 pandemic, the issues brought forth by the lecture speakers remain as salient as ever. Our hope is that this book, as with its predecessor, continues to shed much insight into the thoughts, aspirations and experiences of children growing up in Singapore. And it will inspire more discussion with the aim of bringing about societal change in the decades to come.

Koh Choon Hui DUBC
Chairman, Singapore Children's Society

Preface

This book was published in celebration of the 70th anniversary of the Singapore Children's Society in 2022. This is the second book to present the annual Singapore Children's Society lectures. The first book was a collection of eight lectures for the years 2007 to 2014. This book comprises six lectures presented from 2015 to 2021. We skipped a lecture in 2020 because of heightened Covid-19 pandemic restrictions. In the tradition of the first book, we introduce the speakers and include their responses to questions raised at the lectures. Taking advantage of the time that has elapsed since the lectures, we interviewed the speakers for their current views on the topic as part of gaining insight into their personal journey. The exception to this was the late Dr John Elliott, for whom we interviewed his former students and colleagues.

The topic of how technology impacts society has never been more relevant today. In the first chapter, Mr Han Fook Kwang reflects on the ways technology has changed our lifestyle, as well as how we communicate, receive and digest information. He contends that there is still a place for newspapers with journalists who can tell stories that connect emotionally with their readers. The liberty to "act freely" within the digital world that Mr Han talks about is a theme we are still meditating on. In this third year with Covid-19, we are certainly grateful for the advent of technologies which permit virtual meetings and asynchronous learning. However, there remains a need to examine the mental health issues arising from the social isolation that many experience and the lack of opportunities young children have for developing social interaction skills. In the era of social media, we reflect that the stress that our children may experience while attempting to "always be seen to be happy and surrounded by beautiful things", in Mr Han's words, are problems that have yet to be sufficiently addressed.

Ms Grace Fu presents her vision for our youths in the second chapter. She posits that our youths need to be curious and interested in the world; they must be willing to try new things and pick themselves up when things do not go to plan. If her message sounds familiar, it is perhaps because speakers in the first book, *Speaking of Children: The Singapore Children's Society Collected Lectures,*[1] had similar advice for parents as well. The suggestion by Mr Janadas Devan, a former journalist and an academic, for parents to let their children explore their surroundings by climbing trees and cycling downhill at high speeds is very

---

[1] *Speaking of Children: The Singapore Children's Society Collected Lectures* is a compilation of the Society's first eight annual public lectures. The book was launched in October 2015.

much in the spirit of Ms Fu's lecture. In the same vein, Mr Ho Kwon Ping, the Executive Chairman of Banyan Tree Holdings, rallied for parents to nurture the curiosity of their children and to encourage them to ask *why*.

In the third chapter, Mr Chan Chun Sing tells us the story of a simple society where the younger generation's accomplishments are measured in ways determined by the older generation. This is not what he envisages for our children. Rather, he hopes that parents can appreciate the strengths and weaknesses of their children, and support their children's development accordingly. His views echo the advice given in the first book by the wordsmith that is Mr Devan, who suggested that parents should not impose their ambitions on their children. Mr Chan similarly wishes for parents to let their children stumble because recovering after stumbling is part of the learning process. In fact, he wants to persuade parents not to "overly protect or bubble wrap" their children. It is, after all, how we develop resilience.

The caseworkers at Singapore Children's Society can attest to the complexities surrounding the difficulties that children from lower-income families face in growing up. As Associate Professor Teo You Yenn eloquently puts it, "we have not paid sufficient attention to the larger social conditions that shape their experiences and options in society". In the fourth chapter of this book, A/P Teo discusses her research findings on social inequality and their impact on children, youths and families. From her recent work on the minimum income standards of local families,[2] she further shares that access to education *and* the resources for keeping up with the academic demands at school are both part of a family's basic needs.

In the fifth chapter, the late Dr John Elliott spoke on topics close to his heart — the importance of considering cultural context

---

[2] Ng Kok Hoe, Teo You Yenn, Neo Yu Wei, Ad Maulod, Stephanie Chok & Wong Yee Lok (2021). *What People Need in Singapore: A Household Budgets Study*. https://whatsenough.sg/key-findings-mis2021/.

when applying theories of parenting and the need for parenting recommendations to be supported by contextualised research. Citing local research on caregiving arrangements and their impact on young children's development, he reassured parents that they need not feel guilty for making grandparents, childcare centres or domestic helpers the main caregivers of their young children. It is one thing to be supported by flexible work arrangements and government schemes which help mothers return to work, as highlighted by Madam Halimah Yacob, the President of Singapore, in the first book. It is another thing to receive assurance that placing young children in the care of trusted adults does not entail poorer developmental outcomes.

The final and sixth chapter of this book deals with children's rights. Mrs Priscilla Lui sets out a systemic framework that marries a multidisciplinary team of professionals with policies and legal statutes that take guidance from the United Nations Convention on the Rights of the Child (UNCRC). Of worth noting, in particular, is that she advocates for the abolishment of corporal punishment, on the grounds that children have the right to be free from physical harm. This continues the theme from the first book, where Professor Leong Wai Kum, an Emeritus Professor of Law at the National University of Singapore, unequivocally argued for the end of corporal punishment across settings in Singapore, in line with the UNCRC.

The speakers of the Singapore Children's Society lecture series across the two books offer their individual perspectives on differentiated topics but yet have overlapping views. They talk about the need for children to experience failure in order to develop resilience and the need for children to take responsibility for their actions by being given opportunities to make decisions, albeit smaller ones at the beginning. The questions raised by the audience overlap on areas concerning systemic and micro-level changes on the topics of parenting, children's well-being and education.

But it is also to be acknowledged that the speakers grew up at a different time. Mr Chan notes that children and youths today have "genuinely different challenges from the previous generation", who grew up with fewer resources. At a time when parents were busy earning a living to look after the family, children naturally did their homework on their own. The curriculum was appropriately matched to their abilities, allowing students to advance through school without external help. However, as A/P Teo reminds us, we are no longer living in the 1970s or the 1980s. The lectures do not hold any easy answers, but they raise awareness of the issues that we are to deal with in the coming years.

Acknowledgements

We are exceedingly grateful to all the speakers for sharing their thoughts, personal history and journey, and their relevant corporate communications teams for their editorial inputs regarding the respective chapters. We are thankful to Lim Lee Ching, Michelle Chiang, Heidi Yeo, Goh Guan Zhen, Joses Kuan and Jolene Ooi for providing their astute inputs on the draft manuscript. We appreciate Anngee Neo's tireless efforts to convert our metaphors of inequality, resilience and Tiger parenting to charming illustrations, and express our gratitude to SPH Media Limited for the use of the photographs in this book.

About Singapore Children's Society and the Lectures

Established in 1952, the Singapore Children's Society protects and nurtures children and youth of all races and religions. With the mission of bringing relief and happiness to children in need, the Society operates more than ten service centres islandwide, offering services in the four categories of: Vulnerable Children and Youth, Children and Youth Services, Family Services and Research and Advocacy. The annual Singapore Children's Society Lecture, which started in 2007, serves to raise awareness among the public as well as professionals working with children and families, on topics concerning the welfare and well-being of children, youth and families.

Contents

CHAPTER ONE

Growing Up in the Digital World

Han Fook Kwang

About the Speaker

Technology changes society, asserted Mr Han Fook Kwang in his lecture *Growing Up in the Digital World*. Having grown up in an age when news moved slowly, adults toiled to support their families in cramped quarters, and parents did not lecture their children about their grades, he believes that schools should be the place of formal education and home the safe haven for children.

His mother, an illiterate village girl from Hainan Island who came to Singapore to marry a man she had never met, loved her children unconditionally. His father, who would write letters to his children while working in Malaysia and away from home, had his own way of showing concern to his children. Typical of an earlier generation where fathers were often reticent and most mothers were full-time caregivers, neither parent helped with his homework, even though both took an interest in Mr Han's schooling.

The unspoken expectations of parents wanting their children to complete schooling to eke out a life better than theirs were nonetheless received by Mr Han and his siblings. His father had once encouraged him in one of his letters, "If you do well in the exams, you never know, you may become the Prime Minister of Singapore." He also observed his father going through his school bag and looking at his exercise books every once in a while. But Mr Han reached a turning point one day when he came home from school with his report book. After witnessing the biggest smile his mother ever had after reading the words "first in class", he was soon resolved to do well in school to make his mother happy.

He went on to read Mechanical Engineering at the University of Leeds under a Colombo Plan scholarship and subsequently obtained a Masters in Public Administration from Harvard University under a Singapore Government scholarship. After spending a decade in the Singapore Government Administrative Service, he joined The Straits Times mid-career, going on to head the Political Desk, and subsequently taking on the role of Editor-in-Chief for yet another decade.

Mr Han is currently the Editor-at-Large at The Straits Times and a Senior Fellow at the S. Rajaratnam School of International Studies, where his research focuses on the Singapore identity, in particular, with regard to how it has changed and how it is evolving.

On the current media scene, he observes that it is a radically different world from when he first joined the newspaper in 1989. There are many more options today for the reader and this has important implications for both consumers and producers of news. While older Singaporeans may still be reading traditional media such as newspapers or watching local television, they also search for news on alternative sites such as The Online Citizen, Mothership and Facebook, to name a few. Younger Singaporeans, in comparison, are often reliant on social media and are averse to paying for news. In response to these trends, and to increase readership, news organisations play up stories that attract the most eyeballs, using technology to achieve their objectives. It is no longer what is the most important news but which will attract the most readers. This tendency has changed the media landscape completely.

In the short space of time between the lecture and now, *fake news*, misinformation and disinformation are now so commonplace, it is hard for readers to discern what is factual and truthful. Mr Han feels the only long term solution is to train young readers, in particular, to think critically about issues, to ask the right questions and to not accept things at face value. He believes Singapore's education system needs to change to be able to do this well. As for newspapers, they need to do a better job

Han Fook Kwang as an 8-year-old.

of connecting with readers at the emotional level and making them feel that the paper understands their concerns and can help them make sense of the complicated world we live in.

The 9th Lecture, delivered 10 October 2015

When Associate Professor John Elliott first asked me in January or February 2015 to do this lecture, I agreed rather hesitantly, even though I had no idea at that time what I would be talking about. A few months later when I was asked what the topic would be, I still hadn't decided, so I replied rather vaguely that it would be about *Growing Up in the Digital World*. You know, there's a very bad habit of journalists because when your editor presses you about what your next column is going to be, we usually mumble vaguely some topic, so as to give us the greatest flexibility to write about whatever we wanted to write.

So I'm going to talk about the digital world today, not as an expert — I'm not an expert on the internet or on the technology that underpins it. What I am interested in is the impact of technology on society, how it changes society and how it will change society in the future.

Let me start with a few stories about the amazing digital world that we have today. The first story comes from the United States. Sometime in February this year, strange photos started appearing on the phone of an American called Matt Stopera. Let me quote exactly what he said when he saw all these photos that didn't belong to him but had suddenly appeared on his photo stream. "I see a ton of pictures I didn't take, most memorably about 20 selfies of some dude and an orange tree. Hilarious and scary." He had no idea. All sorts of thoughts raced through his mind. Had his phone been hacked? Maybe it had been possessed by some spirit, as some strange photos started appearing? He told this to a friend of his, and the friend understood completely what was happening.

His friend told him that his phone was in China and the man in the photo was still logged on to his iCloud. For those of you who don't know what iCloud is, it is a service that you can subscribe to;

you can store your data, your documents and your photos. You don't have to store these on your iPhone or on your laptop. The service enables you to store your photos remotely. It was launched by Apple in 2011. So, when his friend told him this, it immediately registered with him — he had lost his phone more than a year ago in a bar in New York. Obviously, this person had his iPhone now and had started taking pictures. And because his old iPhone is still registered with his Apple account, with his iCloud account, all the photos that this man in China has been taking is now appearing on Matt Stopera's new phone in America.

Matt Stopera happens to be an online journalist, so he started writing about this story. The title of this story was *Who is this man and why are his photos showing up on my phone?*[1] and he posted it on this website called BuzzFeed, which is one of the biggest websites in the US. So, he thought, "Okay, I did my story. End of story." But it wasn't the end of the story because within hours of posting the story he was getting all sorts of tweets and postings from China. What happened was that his post had been translated into Chinese and posted on the Chinese social media website called Weibo and he was receiving all sorts of messages. Let me give you a few examples. The first one says, "I'm Chinese and in our country we are trying to find this man. You are famous in China now." And the second one says, "My friends and I are making an effort to find the *orange tree guy*." And another says, "Haha, right after you tweeted on Weibo, your name is now trending at number one, out of 100 hot search rankings." And so within hours, he was actually the biggest topic in Weibo; he was trending at number one. Weibo is huge. It's like Facebook in the

---

[1]See also Matt Stopera, "How I became a minor celebrity in China (After my stolen phone ended up there)". *BuzzFeed*, 21 February 2015. https://www.buzzfeed.com/mjs538/how-i-became-a-minor-celebrity-in-china-after-my and "I followed my stolen iPhone across the world, became a celebrity in China, and found a friend for life". *BuzzFeed*, 1 April 2015. https://www.buzzfeed.com/mjs538/i-followed-my-stolen-iphone-across-the-world-became-a-celebr#.iux0vRMaKk.

US. And of course, given the power of social media, within an hour or so, somebody said, "We found him, the *orange tree guy*, haha. The internet is amazing. Maybe someone will help you contact him."

To cut a long story short, because they found *Orange Brother*, Matt Stopera started messaging *Orange Brother*, and they arranged for Matt to visit him in China. Because Matt works for BuzzFeed, which is a very big company, the company sponsored his trip to China. Before long, Matt Stopera was in China and he became a celebrity there. When he arrived at the airport, there were hundreds of journalists and he eventually met *Orange Brother*. Well, we shouldn't call him *Orange Brother* because he has a name, Mr Lee Hong Chung. Matt Stopera was all over China. He launched all sorts of products. He opened shops. He visited Mr Lee's hometown in Meizhou. Within a week, they became the new faces of US-China relations.

I thought it is an amazing story because it has all the elements of the digital world. The technology is simply amazing, this service called iCloud, where you can save your photos. The digital world has this ability to connect people. Matt and Lee, they don't speak the same language. Matt doesn't speak a word of Chinese and Lee doesn't speak a word of English, but they are able to connect across language, across culture and obviously across geography.

The second story I'm going to tell is a very different story. It's about young boys and girls in a military-style boot camp in China. There are more than 600 million internet users in China. It has been reported that about 24 million of them are young people who are addicted to the internet. These young boys and girls have been sent to the boot camp by their very worried and anxious parents because their children are addicted to the internet.

And by addicted, I mean they spend eight to ten hours online, disregarding everything, their schoolwork, their family life and so on. Their parents have simply given up and actually don't know what to do. So, these young people are being sent to this camp. They go through a very tough regime. They wake up at 6.30 am. They do all sorts of physical exercise. They go through psychological testing and counselling and so on. You really don't want to end up in a place like this. That's another aspect of the digital world. It obviously raises all sorts of health and social issues, as well as other issues. I mean, this is a very controversial treatment. Many people are against this and say it doesn't work, but it exists in China.

I thought I should also share with you a story from Singapore, since we are obviously very much a part of the digital world. What happened was, a young South Korean Taekwondo instructor was visiting Singapore at the invitation of the Singapore Taekwondo Federation. While he was in Singapore, he boarded a bus, and while he was on the bus, he saw an old lady who was barefooted. He took pity on her. He approached her and offered her his own slippers. And of course, she was very overcome with emotion and started tearing up. His friend, who was also on the bus, took a picture and uploaded it on the Singapore Taekwondo Federation website. Somebody took that photo from the website and posted it onto the citizen journalism website called Stomp, which is part of Singapore Press Holdings (SPH), which I belong to. Within minutes, it went viral and became a big story, and the newspapers picked it up.[2] And for once a foreigner in Singapore got all sorts of positive comments, not negative ones. The reason why I picked this story is that it shows the power of an image in

---

[2] Walter Sim, "South Korean's kind gesture generates online buzz". *The Straits Times*, 8 February 2013. https://www.straitstimes.com/singapore/south-koreans-kind-gesture-generates-online-buzz.

the digital world, how it can go viral so quickly, and how it can move people so powerfully.

Here are some random, interesting facts about the digital world. When you do a Google search, it immediately sends the query to over 1,000 computers, and within 0.2 seconds, you get not just one answer but sometimes 100,000 answers. A hundred billion emails are sent a day, and one million babies have been born from people who met at Match.com, an online dating website. For those of you who are interested in YouTube, *Gangnam Style* by Psy was the most viewed YouTube video in 2012 when it garnered over 2.4 billion views.

For me, these stories tell us a few things about the digital world. First of all, how amazing the technology is, and how mind-boggling it is. In fact, most of us don't quite understand how it works. How is it that when you do a Google search, in less than a second, 0.2 seconds, you can get 100,000 answers? I can't figure out how it works. How does iCloud work? How do you store your photos and data on this so-called "cloud" remotely on a server? And when you want to recall a photo, you get it immediately? There are lots of technologies that we don't understand, like nuclear technology and brain surgery. But we don't use these technologies every day. In contrast, we use digital technology every day, and not just every day, but sometimes every minute of the day. But for most of us, we don't really understand it. The second point about these stories is the amazing way in which they connect people. The US-China story is a fantastic example of it. I don't think that we have ever experienced in human history the ability to connect so many people so quickly and in such a short space of time. This has important implications in business, in politics and in society, in general. The third point I would like to make is that actually what we are interested in, what really grabs our interests, is the human dimension of the stories, the power of the image and how we are moved as human beings. The technology actually takes a backseat.

> **Question: Given that we have to sort of manage new technology, what key areas would you suggest we include in education to help children and youths better understand and cope with this digital world, assuming the older generation can teach the younger generation?**
>
> **Answer:** I'm not sure you can. First of all, you should never get an older person to teach a younger person because you don't understand it as well as they do. We have many *digital natives* who have grown up in this digital world and who'll go on to be in the position to impart their knowledge and shape society in a way that will benefit society. We are in a transitional world where those in authority, whether they are politicians, media owners or editors, are not *digital natives*. They are struggling with technology; they do not have the answers. But when the transition is complete, I think it will be a different world. With people whose understanding is much deeper shaping society, solutions will be different. The solutions we presently have are responses from people who do not have that understanding.

Technology changes society. The society responds to it and, depending on how the society responds to it, the technology then changes again and adapts to those changes that it has made on that society. So, it carries on. It is an iterative process. The two have a great impact on each other. Let me talk about this in one area that maybe I can claim some expertise in because I have been in this business for 26 years now, which is the media world. When I joined The Straits Times in 1989, obviously it was a very different world. There was no internet, there wasn't even cable television. You couldn't get CNN or BBC. But that was the golden period of the newspaper world. We were, I suppose, a monopoly in Singapore — you had to read The Straits Times, and if you didn't like The Straits Times, too bad! Our sales, our readership and our advertising revenue grew every year, regardless of what we did in the newspaper. Life as a journalist was very simple. You'd write for the next day's paper. If a story broke in the morning, you'd have an entire day to write because the newspaper only appeared the next morning, unlike today. Today, if the news breaks, you'd have to write immediately and you'd need to tweet about it, because people expect the news on their phones. Life for readers was also very simple. You'd read the paper in the morning and, if you hadn't finished reading the paper in the morning, when you returned home in the evening you'd continue reading the paper. That's what my father did. Every morning I saw him reading the paper in the morning, then when he came back, he would lie in bed to read the paper at night. Of course, the news also moved very slowly because nothing much happened between morning and evening.

In fact, it moved so slowly that, I'll give you one example: when the Titanic sank in 1912, many papers got the story wrong the next morning. This was the typical headline in the papers, *Titanic Sinking; No Lives Lost.*[3] The reason why they got it wrong was that, in those days, you could only make contact with a ship out at sea through Morse code — those dots and dashes they sent as electrical signals. What happened was that someone sent a message asking, "Are the Titanic passengers safe?" It was a question mark. The person then received a message that read, "The ship is being towed to Halifax and everyone is okay." The only problem was that this second message was not about the Titanic. It was about another ship being towed, but this person didn't know that. So, he sent the reply to the papers, and this was what we had. Of course, today, if a ship sinks in the middle of the ocean, within seconds you'd get Twitter feeds and Facebook updates, not from journalists but from passengers on the ship. It is the speed at which news moves today that is most significant. This is what distinguishes the digital world from the non-digital world. And it is creating all sorts of problems for politicians and newsmakers all over the world because they can't cope with the speed at which news moves these days.

[3] See Jack Dearlove, "How the sinking of the Titanic was reported". *Journalism.co.uk*, 13 April 2015. https://www.journalism.co.uk/news-features/titanic-disaster-anniversary-how-it-was-reported/s5/a548774/.

When I look back at those early days, it seems like ancient history, but actually, it was only about 20 years ago that there was no internet. In fact, I remember being on an assignment in China, where we wrote our stories while accompanying the Ministers on official trips and we had to file our stories the night before. There was no internet; we couldn't just write our stories and email them back home. What we had to do was use the phone in the hotel room, the one with the handset. We had to strap the handset onto a contraption which we had to bring along, hook onto our computer, which was a huge, massive thing, and then dial in to the Singapore office.

The only problem — you'd take only a few minutes to send the story electronically through the telephone handset in the hotel room — was that in those days, there were telephone operators, who I suspect were listening to our conversation. So, when they heard all these strange electronic noises because the story was being transmitted, they would think that something was wrong and would cut the connection. You would literally hear them shouting, "Wait, wait, what is happening?", and then your transmission would get lost and you would have to do it all over again. The other thing that usually happened was that after every phone call, you would get a knock on the hotel room door, and somebody would appear at the door with the phone bill because they expected you to pay the phone charges immediately.

Those were the good old days, as I said. Then, of course, everything changed with the internet, and our entire publishing world was completely turned on its head. The reason is that it was very, very expensive to do publishing in the old world. The printing presses that we have, we still do have, cost hundreds of millions of dollars. You need to run a newsroom and hire expensive journalists. If you are a television station, you need to buy expensive cameras, studios and radio stations. The internet completely changed that. Because all you need now is a laptop and a broadband connection, and you can reach out to thousands, and, if you're good, to hundreds of thousands of users. You don't need the printing presses; you don't need people to deliver the paper. From being very expensive to reach out to readers, it now becomes dirt cheap and anyone can do it.

The previous communication mode was *one to many*, one newspaper to many readers. Now it has become *many to many*, with many bloggers, writers and photographers reaching out to many people. The experts say that this is the most revolutionary period in the publishing and media world since the invention of the printing presses in the 17th century. And I believe that they are absolutely right. So, how did media companies like SPH, The New York Times and The Times respond to this? I think the first response was almost fatal. Some experts call it the *original sin* which we are still recovering from, which is that the newspapers decided to load everything on the internet for free. Because all these bloggers and other people were giving away their content for free, the media companies also did it in the hope that they would draw readers in and, with many readers in, they would be able to make money from online advertising. But that didn't happen. Online advertising didn't grow and didn't replace the revenue they lost from the print side.

What it did do was merely encourage a free culture online. Everybody now expects to get content free. Very few people are prepared to pay for content online. It destroyed many newspapers, especially in the US and Western Europe. This free culture also resulted in the proliferation of what are called *news aggregators*. These organisations do not have journalists or newsrooms; they do not produce original content. What they do is that they get other people's content and put it on their website. Organisations like Yahoo News and Google, hundreds of them, started doing this. At first, much of the selection of news was from real people, but now with technology, many use computers to curate the news, and they have fancy algorithms to do this.

In fact, one of the most serious challenges that many newspapers face is from Facebook. They have a feature called *News Feed* in which you can get news on whatever your interest is; you can get all sorts of news from all over the world. It is very convenient and you can read the news on your phone. These people are very ambitious and this is what Mark Zuckerberg, the founder of Facebook, says, "Our goal is to build the perfect, personalised newspaper for every person in the world. We are trying to personalise it and show you the stuff that's going to be the most interesting to you."[4] But Facebook doesn't have any journalists. It doesn't spend money. It uses other people's content. So, how did all this affect the newspaper business?

Digital advertising has been growing very rapidly whereas print advertising has been declining. But the thing about digital advertising is that it is not the newspapers which are getting the share of this digital advertising. If it was, then we would be back in business. But it is organisations like Google, Facebook and YouTube which are getting the bulk of this advertising. Media platforms have also changed over the years. Young people typically get their news online and on their mobile phones. They rely less on television and even less on newspapers, whereas older people aged above 60 years still rely quite strongly on mainstream media.

Maybe I should poll the audience. How many of you read the newspapers this morning? Put up your hands. All 60-plus years old! I hope you will pardon me for this quote. This is not from me. This is from Rupert Murdoch who is the biggest publishing tycoon in the world. He was once quoted as saying, "All those reading newspapers are heading for the graveyard; all those reading news online are heading towards college." For newspapers, these are very challenging times. I believe that there is light at the end of the tunnel, but you need to do it well. What newspapers need to do is make sure that they develop and build on

---

[4] See Eugene Kim, "Mark Zuckerberg wants to build the 'Perfect Personalized Newspaper' for every person in the world". *Business Insider*, 7 November 2014. https://www.businessinsider.com/mark-zuckerberg-wants-to-build-a-perfect-personalized-newspaper-2014-11.

their core strength, which is their credibility and brand recognition. You can't quite trust what you read on the web if it is by some blogger or some unknown person. But hopefully you can trust what you read in The Straits Times because we are 170 years old and we've been around for a long time.

With so much information online and so much noise out there, it is even more important, I believe, that newspapers continue to make sure that they are the most trusted and reliable source of information. I would argue that it is very important for society to make sure that newspapers survive because mainstream media and news organisations are the only organisations that have the resources to create original content. The other people are just taking the content for free. We are the only people in the world who can send reporters to Iraq or Afghanistan or, in our part of the world, to Kalimantan or Sumatra to find out who is burning all those fires in the forest. Nobody else can do it.

Let me hasten to add before you all leave this room and think that The Straits Times is in serious trouble. We are still a highly profitable newspaper. In fact, we are probably one of the most profitable in the world. We are doing much better than many other newspapers around the world largely because of our very dominant position in Singapore. But at the same time, the forces that are impacting them are impacting us as well — the pervasiveness of the internet, the widespread use of mobile phones and the fact that young people these days are no longer reading the papers as much as people used to.

Of course, the media world isn't the only industry that is affected by all the changes that technology has brought about. Many other businesses have also been revolutionised and turned upside down. Some of these you are quite familiar with. Organisations like Amazon and eBay have completely changed the retail business. In music, iTunes has almost decimated the Compact Disc (CD) industry. HMV has closed down because they can't survive. Nobody is buying CDs anymore. In photography, Kodak has disappeared because everybody is using digital cameras these days. Even digital cameras are facing severe challenges and sales have come down because you can now take pictures with your phone. And the camera in your phone is so sharp these days. It is almost as good as having a standalone digital camera. So, even digital cameras might disappear one day.

Some of the businesses that have emerged are, in my mind, very counterintuitive. Uber is a good example. Uber is a private hire car business which is challenging the taxi industry, but if you had asked me a few years ago whether it would do well, I would have said, "Oh, would you trust having somebody pick you up, somebody whom you don't know, in a private car, who is not registered as a taxi driver? He might be more interested in your taxi fare, for all you know." But Uber has grown incredibly. It has attracted USD1.2 billion in venture capital. And Uber is now valued at USD18 billion. Of course, I think, the trick is that it does many things that you can't do with a taxi apparently. I have not used Uber, but I'm told you can actually watch, on your phone, the car as it makes its way to pick you up, so you know exactly when it is going to pick you up. You can't do that with a taxi. And you don't pay cash to the Uber driver; you pay through credit card to the company. Plus you can actually read what other people say about the driver and how they rate him. So, before you click *Agree* to that driver picking you up, you can read all the reviews, and if everybody says, "Wow, what a fantastic driver he is" and so on, then I suppose you can trust the verdict of the crowd out there. If so many people say he is a good driver, then what's the problem?

The other business which is as counterintuitive is Airbnb. This is a website in which you can let your house, your home, be used by someone visiting your country. And also, if you are visiting, let's say London, you can use somebody else's home. Again, I would think it is very counterintuitive. How many people would allow total strangers to stay in their home? And how many would want to live in somebody else's home? But Airbnb has 1.5 million houses listed on its website, including 1,400 castles. In fact, I was just reading yesterday about some Singaporeans who paid about $120 for a night at an Airbnb in London, which is a third of the cost of a hotel room, which is say $300 a night. And again, there are user reviews. Before you agree to stay in somebody's house in London, you can read about what all the other people who have stayed in that person's house have to say about their experience — that the bedroom was fantastic and so forth.

The most revolutionary and successful is Facebook. It has 1.4 billion active users and when the initial public offering was made a couple of years ago, it attracted USD16 billion in capital. Again, I wouldn't have thought that so many people would be willing to share so much of their personal information with so many other people. I couldn't have imagined that you could make a business out of it. It is one of the most successful digital companies in the world. Let me read you a joke that a person wrote, "I haven't got a computer, but I was told about Facebook and Twitter, and I'm trying to make friends outside of Facebook and Twitter, while applying the same principles. Every day I walk down the street and tell whoever passes by what I have eaten, how I feel, what I have done the night before and what I will do for the rest of the day. I give them pictures of my wife, my daughter, my dog and me gardening and on holidays, spending time by the pool. I also listen to their conversations and tell them I like them and give them my opinion on every subject that interests me, whether it interests them or not. And it works. I already have four people following me — two police officers, a social worker and a psychiatrist!"

What do people do on social media? Most people use social media to find out what their friends are doing and to connect with them, as well as send messages directly to them. I've spent some time discussing the business world because it is the business world which is really driving the digital world. It's only businesses — not governments, social organisations or non-governmental organisations — that have the resources, the people and the talent to invest in technology. It is in the interest of businesses to want to connect as many people as possible and to make the technology even better and faster. They want to dominate the digital world because, in the digital world, size is almost everything. I read somewhere that the top ten websites in the US account for 75% of all the internet traffic. They include familiar names like Google, YouTube and Facebook. There are some Chinese names in there too because, on the internet, Chinese companies like Baidu and Tencent are also very big.

But it's not what the businesses do that interests me. It's what they do to society and how society responds that interests me. It's also what they uncover about human behaviour and the responses that we might otherwise never have been aware of that interest me, such as the willingness to share personal details or to trust total strangers. When businesses impact society, they also throw out certain issues. And I want to turn to some of those issues now, particularly two issues. One is the loss of privacy; the other is the way we receive information or what some people call the *filter bubble*.

First, let me deal with the loss of privacy and identity. I've talked about Facebook, but let me give you some other examples. There is a geospatial analysis platform called Google Earth, which you can use to look at almost every house, even in Singapore, from space. There's also a software called Zillow. I'm not sure if it's available in Singapore, but in the US you can use it to find out the number of bedrooms in a house, where the bathrooms are, the floor area and how much that house is worth.

We think that only the police have our fingerprints. But digital cameras are so powerful and sharp these days that if I take a picture of you and your palms are clearly visible, I can capture your fingerprints and build up a database of fingerprints from other people as well. Facial recognition is another technology that is quite amazing. If you have a picture of someone, there's a software which you can use to search the entire Facebook around the world to identify this person. And because you've identified him through Facebook, you can get all his personal details from Facebook. All you need is a picture. You don't need his name and his other details. But of course, the people with the most information about you are actually companies that want to sell you things. Because every time you visit a website, whether it is to read stuff or buy things, you leave traces of your identity there. And the people who are interested in that information will know what other websites you have visited and what you have bought. If you have a Facebook account, they will know all sorts of other things about you too.

So it's possible to get that information if you want to. And there are companies which want to sell that information to other companies which are interested to sell you things. In fact, there's a new kind of advertising online called programmatic ads and these ads follow you online. Even if you and your wife are visiting the same website, let's say if you're both reading The Straits Times online, the two of you will be looking at very different advertising. It's not like in the physical newspaper. If you're reading The Straits Times, you'll see the same ads. But online, you'll be seeing different ads. Your wife may be seeing ads about shoes and dresses, whereas you may be looking at ads on gadgets, the latest handphones to buy or books and so on. And the reason why they are able to do it is that, as I mentioned earlier, they have found out a lot about you based on the websites that you have previously visited. They know that your wife is interested in shoes. The shoe company which wants to sell your wife shoes is willing to pay money to target its ads. It will specify for the website to show ads to only women between the ages of 35 and 40 who bought shoes in the previous year. If such a person happens to visit the website, the ad will be delivered to her.

In the digital world, almost nothing is lost. It's all there. It's all stored or archived, waiting for the next person to look at it. Whatever you have posted online — maybe you did something silly when you were 7 years old and you posted a picture of it — it will still be there when you are 70 years old. And anybody who is interested in it can search for it. Do people worry about this loss of privacy? I think most people are resigned to it. Most people have the attitude that, "Well, what can I do about it? I want to go online. I want to buy things. I want to do all these wonderful things in the digital world, so what can I do?"

Psychologists say that many of us are what they call *eternal optimists*, meaning that even if we are worried about what people might do with the information they have about us, we are optimistic. We say that bad things won't happen to us; they will happen to the next person so we'll just carry on as such. The benefits outweigh the cost. But there are some people who are worried. Alessandro Acquisti, a Professor from Carnegie Mellon University, says, "What I fear is the normalisation of privacy invasions in a world where we become so adjusted to being public in everything that it is normal. I fear that that world will be a world where we will be less human. Part of being human is having a private sphere and things you only share with special people, or with no one. I fear for the future of that world."[5] He may be putting it in the extreme sense, but I think that there is something there that's worth our while to think about.

The other issue I want to talk about is the information that we get from the internet or the digital world. You might think that when you search for something online, the answers you get come from a very neutral, sort of objective search, but actually that is not the case. In fact, this is an experiment that was carried out: when two people did a Google search for Egypt the country, they got quite different answers, or at least for their first 20 to 30 answers, the ones that you are most likely to read. The first person who searched for Egypt got all the political websites because he was

---

[5] Bob Sullivan, "Why should I care about digital privacy?". *NBC News*, 10 March 2011. https://www.nbcnews.com/id/wbna41995926.

doing the search at a time when there were all these problems in Cairo with the Arab Spring and Mubarak being overthrown. So, he got all the political news. The second person who was not at all interested in politics got all the tourist information — what to visit in Cairo, the top ten things to do in Egypt and so on. This happens because the search engines are very clever in giving you answers they believe you are interested in. Because the more they tailor their answers to what is relevant or interesting to you, the more people will visit their website. Because their answers are relevant. They have very, very clever algorithms for doing that.

Is this a good thing? Well, if you are in their business, like Mark Zuckerberg of Facebook, then it is a good thing. He was famously quoted saying, "A squirrel dying in your front yard may be more relevant to your interest right now than people dying in Africa." Facebook has lots of talented people working on their algorithms to deliver information which they believe you are personally interested in, not what is most important or significant, but what is most interesting and relevant to you.

On the other hand, there are some people who are quite worried about this. This person called Eli Pariser wrote a book called *The Filter Bubble*.[6] He worries about it because he says that, if the internet — or if what you read or search on the internet — only gives you what you are interested in or what you believe in, then your worldview will become increasingly narrow. This is because you're only reading things that you're interested in or believe in, which are in sync with your own ideology, beliefs and interests. You will never be fed things which you are not interested in, even though they may actually be more important than the things which you are fed with. He believes that this *filter bubble* has the possibility of undermining civic discourse and making people more vulnerable to propaganda and manipulation.

---

[6] Eli Pariser, *The Filter Bubble: What the Internet is Hiding from You* (London: Penguin Books, 2011).

Question: What are your thoughts on the positive impact of *digital natives*? What are the challenges or consequences that may develop from having our children grow up in the digital world?

Answer: I'm not sure I'm the best person to comment on this. Because when my children were young, I was very worried about their use of the internet. So, I said, "No computer in the bedroom; all computers must be in the living room." I think it only lasted for about two or three years. They said, "Oh, it's not convenient. We need to do our homework with it. The living room has all sorts of distractions." Then I imposed another rule. With computers in the bedroom, I had less control so I fixed a timer onto my router, and the timer would switch off the router at 10 pm. It worked for a while until my daughter raised hell and said, "You're depriving me of the oxygen that I need to do all this research and schoolwork!"

As parents, we do worry about what our children use the internet for. But I believe that the solution comes from the non-digital world. How we raise our children, how we impart values that will help them do well in life and how confident our children are about their relationship with us — these are not matters that concern the digital world directly. But I believe the stronger our relationship and the more we do the right things in the non-digital world, the better our children cope with the digital world.

I know some people have all sorts of rules. Some people believe that you should not allow children to have their own computers in the bedroom; all computers must be in the living room so that you can control not just the time they spend on computers but also what they do on the computer. Other people believe you need to install filters.

But children know more about the digital world than we do; they can find all sorts of ways to get around filters. I have great confidence — I'm very optimistic and positive, frankly — in the abilities of the young to manage and navigate this world. I think it belongs to them. That's why there's the term *digital native*. We are what they call *digital immigrants*, like foreign talent. We are not natives; we have to learn and grow up and be integrated into that society.

Let me now try to pull everything together. The ability of the digital world to connect people, I believe, will become even greater in the future because there are many big businesses interested and motivated in making it even more interconnected. It is their business model: the more people connect through Google, Facebook, Uber and Airbnb, the bigger their businesses and greater their business opportunities are.

In the future, we will see more amazing technologies which will enable people to be connected even more quickly. I've tried to show you that when this happens, certain issues will be thrown up, issues about privacy and about what sorts of information you get. How society responds to those issues will determine how those issues will be resolved. To take a very simple example, if everybody were disgusted and against the sharing of so much personal information online, then I don't think Facebook or social media would have developed the way they did. Obviously there wasn't such a reaction, so Facebook and Google thrived. The people who will resolve these issues are not the technical people. It will not be the software engineers or even the business people. It will be the users of Facebook and Google, people like you and me. So, how we respond to technology will determine how technology unfolds. And when we confront some of these issues and resolve them, ultimately we will come to the core of the issue, which is our identity in the wider context of the community and the society.

We have a powerful tool — the digital world. So, how do we use it? Do we use it just to amuse ourselves, to look at all these websites, to buy things and to book our holidays? Or do we use it to understand ourselves better? Do we use it to understand the society we live in and the people in other societies? The technology doesn't provide us with the answers. It's society, you and me, and the way we use the technology that will decide.

Finally, I think that growing up in the digital world gives us enormous capacity to act freely, to be autonomous individuals, to have the freedom to do things we are interested in and connect with people who are interested in the same things. Some people say that this search for autonomy is in fact the defining character-

Four-year-olds taking part in a coding programme. The children are learning how to operate PETS, a friendly Japanese wooden robot that teaches the basics of computer programming. *Source*: The Straits Times © SPH Media Limited. Reprinted with permission.

istic of modern society. We want to be free to do things, to be freed from the rigid constraints of tradition, custom or society. Whether or not we have the internet, we are a modern society. But the internet empowers us to exercise our freedom to a much greater extent than ever before in human history. There is some research to show that, the more you value freedom, the more you use the internet. And the more you use the internet, the more autonomous you become. This enables you to act in all the different areas that you are interested in, whether it is business, the media, politics or civil society and so on. And it is a positive thing because it expands your sense of personal security. It expands your level of personal freedom. It expands your ability to influence other people.

All these factors are what the researchers have found to be factors which greatly expand your level of personal happiness. The internet is a great contributor to that culture of autonomy. But at the same time, there is also a lot that we do not know about the impact of the digital world on society. In fact, we often misread the impact of these changes. This isn't surprising because we are in the relatively early stages of this digital revolution. It's like the invention of the printing presses or books. At that time, there were many people who were worried about the written word being so freely available to so many people and the sorts of damage it might do to human society.

Even in Singapore, concerns have been raised about online public discussions where it is usually anonymous; all sorts of things can be said. If you were to go by what you read on social media, you would never have expected the ruling party — the People's Action Party (PAP) — to do as well as it did in the General Election (GE). In fact, if you'd been reading only social media, you would have expected the opposition to have done better than it did.[7] It shows how little we understand the internet, its impact and how people respond to it. I believe that as the technology evolves and as we become more adept at it, we will develop a deeper understanding, but only if we discuss these issues. I've raised some of these issues, but there are many other issues out there. I hope that my presentation will have contributed a little to that understanding.

---

[7] There is a backstory as to why Mr Han mentioned this. His original lecture date was set on 11 September 2015, but it coincided with polling day for the GE that year, and the lecture was postponed to 10 October 2015 instead. The GE 2015 marked a significant year for the PAP, which won 83 out of the 89 contested seats. They also gained 69.9% of the popular vote, an increase of 9.8% from the previous election in 2011.

Question: There is research showing that people are becoming more distracted and forgetful as they spend more time online and, as a result of excessive usage, people's attentiveness, memory and ability to engage in deep thinking get affected as well. In recent years, schools are increasing the usage of technology in classes, encouraging our children to use more of the internet to gather knowledge and information. What is your take on balancing the benefits of increasing usage with the perils to a diminished style of thinking and capacity for depth that might result?

Answer: I've read some of it. And there is also research to show that there's a difference when you read a book compared to when you read something online, whether on your tablet or phone. There are two different sorts of behaviours in response to the medium. The research purportedly shows that when you read a physical copy of something, you tend to retain the context of what you have read better than when you read it online.

Maybe there is some truth in it, especially in the case of newspapers. Because when you're reading the newspaper, the paper has your undivided attention. It's the only thing in front of you, so you read it; whereas if you're reading something online, you can be doing all sorts of other things. You can be opening multiple windows. You can be answering an email. You can be looking at somebody else's Facebook account, and then reading whatever you're reading. You're multitasking. They say that young people are very good at multitasking, whereas older people can only do one thing at a time, right?

There's also research which shows that it depends on what you are reading. There is research which says that if you are reading fiction, then it doesn't matter whether you're reading it in the book form or if you're reading it on a tablet. But if you are reading non-fiction, such as a report, then when you are reading it in the printed form, somehow you either remember it better, or it triggers off more analytical thinking than when you are reading it online. To be fair, I've also read other research which shows that it's not true that you don't read deeply when you are reading online. We are in the relatively early period of this digital revolution and we are still coming to terms with it. We still don't know all the answers. I don't think many of the experts have very conclusive findings as well. There is a lot of research being done and, as we understand technology and these issues better, hopefully we will come to better terms with it.

I believe that technology is a very positive force for knowledge and learning. In my line of work where I need to write, and I need to do a lot of research on some of the topics I write about, I can't imagine how I could have functioned 20 years ago. During then, when we wanted to do research, we would go to the little library in SPH. We would maybe ask the librarian to do the research for us, but it was very slow. Today, I can just Google for answers on the internet. It's an incredible invention and it's really up to us to make use of it.

All of us have to embrace it. All of us have to find our own little balance between the digital and the non-digital world. I have great confidence in human society and its ability to adapt and to make use of that technology.

CHAPTER TWO

Our Children, Their Hopes and Future

Grace Fu

About the Speaker

Having been brought up in a resolutely matriarchal family, Ms Grace Fu's view of a woman's role in society has very much been influenced by the role models in her life. Her grandmother, Mdm Liew Yuen Sien, was the longest-serving principal of Nanyang Girls' High School, and her mother worked full-time as a nurse at the then Kandang Kerbau Hospital (now known as KK Women's and Children's Hospital). Ms Fu herself has held a number of senior positions in the government, even becoming the first female full Minister in Singapore to helm her own Ministry in 2015.

Ms Fu is the current Minister for Sustainability and the Environment (MSE). She obtained an Honours degree in Accountancy and a Masters of Business Administration from the National University of Singapore. After working in the areas of corporate planning, financial control and business development, she went on to helm the Port of Singapore Authority Southeast Asia as its Chief Executive Officer. She entered politics in 2006 when she was elected as a Member of Parliament for the Group Representation Constituency of Jurong, Yuhua Division.

Ms Fu was the Minister for Culture, Community and Youth (MCCY) when she delivered the lecture *Our Children, Their Hopes and Future*. Over the years, she has held various ministerial positions at the Ministry of National Development, the Ministry of Education, the Ministry of Foreign Affairs and the Ministry of Information, Communications and the Arts, as well as the Ministry of the Environment and Water Resources. Ms Fu has also previously held official roles as the Leader of the House and Minister in the Prime Minister's Office.

In the 2016 National Youth Survey, young people expressed their desire for a comfortable life. Noting this at the time of the lecture and six years on, Ms Fu thinks that our youths should have a more enterprising spirit, especially when compared to peers in other countries who have bigger appetites for risk and uncertainty. She hopes for our youths to be less averse to failure. While she understands the inclination parents have for wanting to step in and resolve the consequences of their children's actions, she also supports letting children take responsibility for their actions and letting them experience failure.

Her belief that our youths should acquire a personal sense of responsibility are not unrelated to her own childhood experiences. Having grown up with a mother who worked long hours as a nurse, she had learnt to be independent from a young age. She recalls that, in her youth, she had to be responsible for her own things as her mother would be busy with her work and domestic matters. When she was unable to find what she needed for school the next day, she would have had to answer to her teacher. In fact, independence and a sense of personal responsibility are traits she has tried to instil in her children.

Overseas trips were a good opportunity to teach her children independence. She would get her children, from when they were about 9 or 10 years old, to routinely navigate new places using physical maps whenever they were overseas. She would also have them pack their own bags and look after their luggage at the airport, and allow them to make their own decisions about how to spend a portion of the money given to them during a trip. Creating a safe space for dinner conversations has also been a way to broach sensitive topics such as current affairs and premarital sex, and their ensuing discussion about legal and personal responsibilities, without parents coming across as nagging.

A holistic education is another issue Ms Fu feels strongly about. She was fortunate that her parents were able to provide her and her siblings with piano, ballet and swimming lessons — opportunities that her mother herself did not have as a child. At that time, having been "fed a routine of things to do from young", she wished she had more leisure time than she did.

It was only later in life that Ms Fu realised the benefits of the holistic education that she received while growing up. When she was helming MCCY, she found that she could appreciate the portfolio more with the background she had gained in sports, dance and cultural activities. The fact that she was given this exposure from young shaped her views on the importance of a well-rounded education. This motivated her

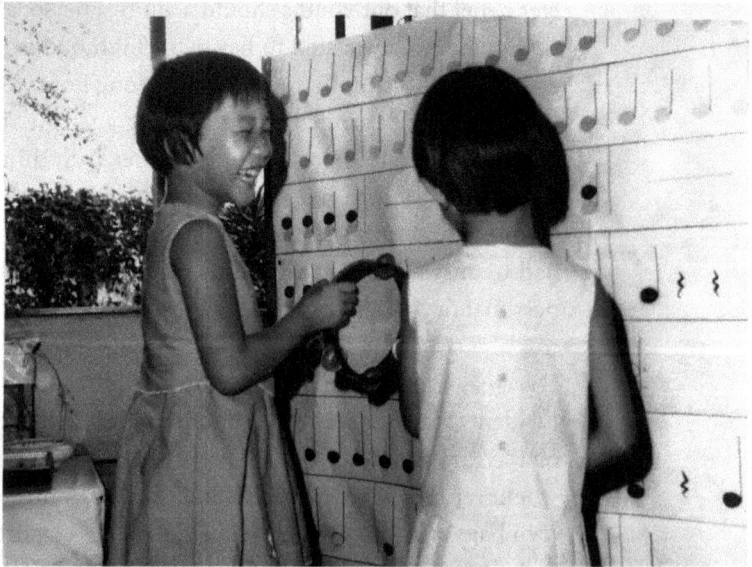

Grace Fu (left), aged 5, attending a kindergarten music class.

to give children more opportunities for experiences outside of studying. She became an advocate for children to experience arts and culture while growing up. She wanted every child to have the opportunity to visit a museum, an art exhibition or a concert hall. "It's not just about listening to a band or an orchestra in your school hall. It's about appreciating it in a hall like the Esplanade or Victoria Theatre, where there is a good system with good sound and good music," she reflected.

In contrast to her own childhood experiences, she gave her sons more room to cultivate their own interests. They were free to choose their co-curricular activity, although she did urge them to choose something sports-related. She feels that learning a sport is a tangible way for children to see themselves achieve something if they put their minds to it and stick to a plan. Through sports, children get to experience success and failure. They invariably learn how to pick themselves up after losing a game. They acquire a sense of fairness and the soft skills for thriving in life — tenacity, discipline, teamwork and drive.

In her lecture, Ms Fu calls for a society with "young people who are resilient and (who) do not fear failure and disruption". This became evident when strict measures to contain the initial spread of Covid-19 were imposed on the public from April to May 2020. Youths took the initiative to support and advocate for the well-being of migrant workers when Covid-19 infections first hit the dormitories. Ms Fu remembers that those were difficult days, when the dormitories recorded large numbers of infections, and the government was moving large numbers of migrant workers to quarantine and community care facilities. Each time the workers went to the facilities, they went with very few belongings and could not go out to buy essential items. Ms Fu was heartened to see youths tapping on their networks to source food and basic necessities like toothbrushes and mattresses for the migrant workers, and commended them for going out of their way to show care and concern for the less privileged in our community.

The 10th Lecture, delivered 8 October 2016

Last year, in 2015, Singapore celebrated its own milestone with SG50. We honoured our pioneers for building Singapore up from the mudflats to a metropolis. They had a vision, worked hard for it, and made it a reality. Singapore is what it is today because of our resilient pioneers, many of whom are here as well. Now, the baton has been passed on to us and to our children to carry on this legacy.

Hence, today, I want to talk about the future and those who will lead us into the next century — our youth, our children. I want to talk about what their dreams are, and what values and attitudes they need to have in order to make these dreams a reality.

Our Youth's Aspirations

We should first ask: what do our youths want?

We do regular surveys on a whole gamut of youth-related issues. In the most recent National Youth Survey,[1] we saw at the top of the list that *maintaining strong family relationships* was the number one life goal, followed by *having a place of my own*. But wait, look further down, and you'll see that *getting married* and *having children* ranked quite a distance lower. Does that mean that they want to stay close to their family emotionally but not physically, and are also not that keen to start a family of their own? At this point in time, I'd like to share an exchange I had with a young entrepreneur. I met Danny Tan of HipVan recently. Danny has been involved in starting up many of these new online businesses

---

[1] *National Youth Survey 2016.* (Singapore: Ministry of Culture, Community and Youth). The survey is a time-series study undertaken by the National Youth Council. It is conducted every few years and examines the major concerns of local youths aged 15 to 34 years in Singapore.

with Zalora and so on, and he started HipVan, which is an online merchandiser for furniture. His aspiration was for it to be the IKEA of the future and at that price point. And I asked him, "Tell me one policy change that you'd like to have." And he said, "You know, we should give young people who are not married a subsidised house." So I said, "Why do you say that?" He said, "Our young people in Singapore, somehow they are very much attached to their family. When we need them to work overtime, they say, 'No, I have to go back and have dinner with my mother. My mother said so.'" And they are worrying too much about maintaining those relationships that perhaps, they are tilting a little bit more towards the *life* part of work-life balance than is desirable for an entrepreneur like him. A few other IT start-up entrepreneurs were there, and they echoed the same sentiments. So, I was quite interested to hear from them further, and when I saw these survey results, again, I think it sort of corroborates what they are saying.

After these first two life goals, next came some of the physiological ones as defined by Maslow — *acquiring new skills and knowledge*, *having a successful career* and *earning lots of money*. *Helping the less fortunate* and *contributing to society* are not in the top five unfortunately, although two out of five said that *helping the less fortunate* and *contributing to society* were important life goals. We also saw that only one in ten youths saw migrating to another country as a very important life goal, which tells us that the vast majority of our youths see Singapore as their home.

In short, our youth want to lead a comfortable life, surrounded by family and friends, in a caring Singapore. What does this survey inform us about the work we need to do at the Ministry of Culture, Community and Youth (MCCY)? How do we prepare our youth for the future given these data points?

Question: I think there's one difference between the older generation of Singaporeans and the younger ones. Nowadays, people make all kinds of cognitive calculations, such as whether they can afford children and so on. But they never had the *cuddle experience*. The older generation, if they were the oldest children, they cuddled their mother's menopausal babies. And then when those babies were growing up, the older siblings had children and they cuddled them. I do think it was a major thing people remembered — a baby as something nice to have around. Of course, they didn't have the responsibility because they were siblings, or they were their siblings' children. I don't know quite how we can deal with this, but I do think it is a real issue that young people today have never cuddled a baby.

On another note, we've got to recognise that fathers love kids and kids need fathers. The economy has recognised motherhood. But it has got to recognise fatherhood too.

Answer: I totally agree with you that the earlier generation has probably had many more opportunities to look after younger brothers, sisters and cousins. A lot more of us were staying together with our extended families. Parents had many more children. Therefore, when they had to work and had children at the same time, work-life balance was, "You are number one, you look after the rest." Right? So that's the generation that was growing up in the 50s and 60s, the *baby boomer* generation's experience there, but I have no solution for this. I don't know how to introduce more babies into the community for young people to carry them. Perhaps the Singapore Children's Society can consider having some sort of cuddling session or something!

I would also say that I agree with you on the part about fathers. The young fathers I've seen are very, very supportive.

They're very involved and very engaged, much more than say, my generation or my parents' generation, and that's a good sign. Because women have to see that this is really a shared responsibility. If women have to carry the sole responsibility of caring for a child, then I think the choice of children or career would be so stark when it has to be made. But if you can do both, knowing that there is more family support, more support from the spouse and that spouses take up some of the load, then I think it will make that journey a lot smoother and more attractive to women.

The Need to be a Global City

First, we need to project into the future and take a view of Singapore's position in the world of the future. What will the future be and how would Singapore be doing? To answer these questions, I will describe two cities.

The first city is one that is disconnected from the world. This city is stable and predictable. Its national identity is fully formed because there are no new influences to affect it. Its labour force is ageing and fossilising. The economy is entirely internal, only serving domestic needs with citizens that only buy and sell goods and services with one other.

Then there is a second city. This is a global city connected to the world, which brings about a certain amount of instability and unpredictability into it. The movement of people in and out of the country brings new ideas and talents, yet disrupts norms and established practices. The internet brings in global influences to challenge current norms and forces the city's identity to adapt. It is exposed to the global marketplace and the accompanying headwinds and competition. Its economy must keep changing to be relevant to the global value chains. Its workforce must continually reskill to be relevant to the marketplace.

It is obvious that the first city model describes very few cities or countries in the world today. And the few that fit the description will not make your list of the most exciting cities to visit or to work in. Such a city will not offer the opportunities or the future that our young people dream of. And it is not a suitable model for us. For a country that has the value of trade several times its Gross Domestic Product (GDP), a country that hosts financial services, legal and accounting services for the region, we cannot pull the plug on the global economy or refuse to participate in it. More importantly, Singapore needs to innovate to grow. And innovation will be disruptive and will require adaptation. Singapore is, in many ways, the city described in the second model. Because of our limited natural resources, our small domestic market and a high standard of living, Singapore needs to continue to be this city.

People in other parts of the world are saying that they want a future that is like the first city — more protected and with less disruption. Perhaps they say this without realising the consequences of it. All over the world, we are seeing politicians, perhaps reflecting the mood of the people, moving away from globalisation and international trade, and towards greater nationalism and protectionism. We saw it with Brexit earlier this year where income inequality (between rural United Kingdom and London, between blue and white collar, and between the educated and the not so), inadequate social services and political disconnect have resulted in an outcome that ultimately divides the society along age lines. Young people want a Great Britain that is part of the European Union, while the rest of the country wants to be great on its own.

The episode offers us many lessons. We want a Singapore that meets the aspirations of all segments of the society and yet thrives in the global economy. Is that possible? It is not an easy undertaking, but it is possible as we have done so in the past decades. Connecting with the populace, understanding aspirations, shaping values and explaining the consequences of our policies are what keep our government busy. I will not delve deeper into this topic as it is not the focus of today's talk. But I would like to register the point that as a responsible government, we do not merely subject to popular wants. We have to provide leadership in steering the populace towards a future with the best outcome and with the most options for our children.

Our surveys tell us our youths face stressors as people elsewhere — uncertainty about the future, uncertainty about jobs, about their financials and about whether they can support their families in the future. They also have to live up to parental expectations, and technological and societal changes have promoted an instant gratification mindset.

How best to prepare our youth to take advantage of our place in the world, to meet the bumpy ride ahead? We need young people who are confident and thrive in uncertainties, who are resilient and do not fear failure and disruptions, who see opportunities amongst challenges and who will create jobs in the future economy.

Our youth must be confident to face the global workforce. They must have the drive to compete and the tenacity to pick themselves up when they fall. They must be lifelong learners and be ready to adapt to new technology and jobs that have yet to be conceived today. They must be able to work in teams, with people of all nationalities and accommodate diversity. Do they have the following qualities?

Preparing our Youths for this Global Future

An Enterprising Spirit

First, *an enterprising spirit*. This means being open to risks, daring to dream and push boundaries, and being confident and resilient enough to chase those dreams.

Our engagements with youths reveal they have certain expectations of the world, expectations that may not mesh with reality. Many are still caught up with pursuing a degree for the degree's sake, when the reality is that skills are what really matter. Those in the workforce expect a predictable and steady rise upwards. However, the reality is that the new economy may be less predictable, with technological and business disruptions requiring the next generation to stay constantly nimble, not set in their ways.

Maybe in the future, human-driven cars will be a thing of the past. Maybe your mail will be delivered by drones. To compete and lead in the new global economy, our youth must be innovative and nimble to take advantage of new opportunities created by evolving technologies and the marketplace.

This is not just true for entrepreneurs. The enterprising spirit is not a vocation, but a frame of mind. You can be an accountant, a nurse, a lawyer or a technician and still carry in you an enterprising spirit. You can always look to see what works and what does not, and strive to learn more and to adjust to make things work better.

And when past opportunities dry up, our youth must be willing to try something new. Their jobs will change and they probably will have to reskill themselves a few times throughout their working lives. They must be open to new experiences and have an attitude of lifelong learning.

The government has taken steps to encourage the spirit of experimentation and resilience by providing resources and opportunities. And here I must pause and say that we are always in a dilemma. Do we provide more and more and more, with the hope that youths will expect less and less and less? Or are we merely reinforcing expectations? It's a very tough choice to make. We have programmes to expose our students to entrepreneurship as early as at the primary school level. We are developing a start-up ecosystem that includes a start-up hub — LaunchPad @ one-north. *SCAPE at Somerset is a vibrant youth hangout that also supports several youth entrepreneurs.

Our Youth Corps Leaders' Programme, which aims to develop 1,000 youth leaders per year by 2018, challenges young leaders to identify, frame and tackle social issues, thus enabling them to apply their problem-solving skills. These real-life experiences give youths a chance to stretch their minds, to make mistakes and to learn. I'll talk more about the Youth Corps Leaders' Programme later.

Our research has also shown that being involved makes one more confident and more willing to contribute to one's community. When we are involved in something larger than ourselves, we develop a sense of belonging and rootedness to our community. So, we should encourage our youths to get out there, explore and get involved in something that they're passionate about and to contribute to the society.

But parents and educators must also change their minds and embrace experimentation in order to let our young take more risks.

Let me give an example that is well known to everyone and that is Yip Pin Xiu.[2] I think most of us would know her journey to sporting excellence has been a tough, long and arduous one. She recently won two Gold medals at the Rio Paralympics. What is less well known is that she is a student at the Singapore Management University. She had taken one year's leave from the university to train full-time and focus fully on swimming. And her performance in the water has inspired the whole nation. Pin Xiu, and her parents, could have taken the established path of pursuing her studies and a job thereafter. Her choice of pathway involved risks and sacrifices. When she first started this journey, the probability of a medal was not as high as it is today. So, when she first started out, like many of our elite athletes, it's a dream goal that they're reaching. And to take that first step, to put aside something that is more established, like a university degree and a job, and go for something that has risk, I think it says something about Pin Xiu. Her choice has given the nation much more.

Her impact will last much longer than the sound of our national anthem *Majulah Singapura* in the stadium. Her impact on the society — on making Singapore more inclusive and inspiring persons with disabilities to take up sports — will go a long way. I am glad that her parents had the courage to support her in her choice to pursue competitive swimming at the expense of her studies. Speaking as someone who's had many discussions with persons with disabilities and their families — many of the families actually take on a more protective stance for their family members with disabilities because of the fear of subjecting them to embarrassment and the stigma of failure. So, for them to take up sports and to be out there competing, with or without a chance of winning a medal, it takes a lot of courage and confidence. This is really what we are trying to illustrate through this example, of

---

[2]Yip Pin Xiu is a Singaporean backstroke swimmer who has muscular dystrophy. She is a five-time Paralympic Gold medallist and the holder of two world records for backstroke events.

someone like Pin Xiu who's put aside an established path to pursue the unknown.

Curiosity

The next attitude that youths must have is to be *curious about the world*. This means that they should be interested in events that are happening around them, in international issues that may affect them, about other cultures, about our culture, about how the world develops around Singapore and how it would have an impact on us. They must be comfortable with diversity and differences. This will provide the knowledge required to operate in the global economy.

When I speak with business leaders, they sometimes tell me that Singaporeans make good middle managers, but to make the breakthrough for the top C positions — the CEOs, the CFOs, the CIOs, the COOs and so on — Singaporeans are less willing to take up an overseas posting or a regional role that requires frequent travelling and managing people from other parts of Asia. Singaporeans thrive in a stable and efficient setting, but lack agility in one that is less so. To be the business head of Asia-Pacific or global companies, you will need to communicate and work with the Chinese, the Vietnamese, the Indonesians and so on. To do so, you need to understand their cultures, their values and attitudes, and their perspectives of things that are shaped by histories and customs. You need to have a finger on the pulse of the geopolitical development in their countries so that you can manage business risks. Many of these skills are not found in textbooks and definitely not in a tuition centre. It will require a curious mind, observant eyes and culturally sensitive speech.

The government supports, for example, through International Enterprise (IE) Singapore, our businesses in venturing abroad. IE Singapore provides rich networks and knowledge about key overseas markets. But learning about all these, about cultural issues, about interpersonal skills and so on, must start from young.

Through our schools, we expose our children and youths to global exchanges and learning journeys. Our cultural institutions, such as our museums, are excellent resources. Many of our primary and secondary school students go on learning journeys to the National Museum of Singapore, the Asian Civilisations Museum, the Singapore Art Museum and the new National Gallery Singapore. The exhibits make history and culture more real and tangible, and students become aware of the wider world and of Singapore's place in it. For instance, at the Asian Civilisations Museum, students learn about the cultures of China, India and our immediate region, and relate these to Singapore's own diverse heritage. This understanding helps them to become confident global citizens.

Parents and educators can influence minds by actively seeking to learn about the world and by bringing learning beyond textbooks and examinable subjects. We should keep ourselves updated on world news and current affairs, and think about how global events will affect us — not only in terms of our economy but also our culture and identity. We have to inculcate this from young and nurture in our youth the curiosity that will make them leaders of the future.

Question: I have a question on preparing children to be open to embracing different cultures, as well as people from different nationalities and different backgrounds. Is it possible to inculcate this quality from very early on say, starting from preschool age? Because at this age children are very much aware of themselves, who they are and where they come from; they can distinguish themselves from other children. It would be good if we can do something at the preschool level to mix children

so that they start early in being open to diversity and being prepared for the future.

Answer: The preschool system is rather stratified, I must say. More so than we would like to see. And because it is not nationalised, the choice of preschool is very much left to the parents, and parents would choose a preschool that fits the learning expectations, outcomes and style that they want for their children. The formal school system, which starts from Primary 1, is where we see a lot more diversity and it's something that we stress quite a lot on, as part of national education or social studies. We celebrate Racial Harmony Day through activities. I think that the message of embracing diversity is consistently sent through the formal school system.

But you are right, the preschool system right now is perhaps less diverse and a lot more protected than I would like. It might be because parents are not having that many babies, so each baby is so precious that you even get parents making a police report when their children get into fights at school. I grew up in a time when the environment was a lot more forgiving and, if you're a child, you'd play and you'd learn by making mistakes. You'd beat a friend and get called out. The teacher would tell you off, and then okay, you'd go back and play again with that friend.

But it's gone. I think the pendulum has swung so much that it's such a protected environment. As a local Member of Parliament, I had this experience of wanting to create a children's playground for a preschool that's in my area, as part of our neighbourhood upgrading. So, I said, "There's this preschool here. Why don't we build a really fascinating playground?" and by that, I mean something that's really close to nature, that's almost mimicking a natural forest environment. People would play around the roots of the trees, play with sand and mud, and so on. The feedback that came back was, "No, no, no. That's too unhygienic and it's too dangerous because the children will trip, and we will have lots of problems with parents." The result was very standard rubber-padded playground equipment because parents would not be able to find fault with this design.

I also experimented with the possibility of a more adventurous playground in another precinct. Again, I had adults coming to me saying, "Look, this is really risky. You should have lots of signs and you should have guard rails around it." I resisted doing that, but I'm still holding my breath. I hope there are no serious injuries there. When that does happen, when there's an injury, we will have to deal with the repercussions. But that's the kind of risk-taking I would like to see. I may not be able to change the attitude of the entire population of parents, but where I can, I will do it in my local area and hope that it will become sort of a norm and that people will agree with me and support my decision.

Sense of Rootedness and Community

The third mindset, in order for Singapore to succeed as a nation, is *a sense of rootedness and responsibility to our community.*

Collectively, we need to think and act as *one Singapore* as we face the future. The successful ones among our youths must contribute to creating jobs in Singapore, leading the rest of Singaporeans and caring for the less successful. I spoke about how in other societies there has been a backlash against globalisation. This happens when there is no shared prosperity. I read an article in The New York Times last week.[3] They interviewed a worker in the Netherlands working for Maersk, a Danish shipping company. He said, "More global trade is a good thing if we get a piece of the cake, but that's the problem. We're not getting our piece of the cake." This is the simple truth. When the gains of global exchange are not felt to be shared fairly, people will feel resentment and anger, and societal bonds will begin to fracture.

Singapore cannot have such a split. The government is committed to ensuring that all Singaporeans benefit from our economic progress although we cannot guarantee equal outcomes. We want all Singaporeans to have equal opportunities and enjoy a decent standard of living. But it is not enough for the government to do this on its own. This must be supported by all Singaporeans.

We are only willing to support each other if we see each other as part of the same family and see Singapore as our shared home. What builds this connection is genuine investment of our time, actions, feelings and emotions in Singapore and other Singaporeans. Each Singaporean must know that they have a stake in Singapore and that they must contribute to it. It is not just a place to visit or reside in, but it is a place to which they have a sense of duty and responsibility.

We have programmes to help our youth form bonds with each other and with society. For example, this year we announced the new National Outdoor Adventure Education Master Plan. As part of this, from 2020, all Secondary 3 students will go through a five-day Outward Bound Singapore (OBS) camp. They will go through individual and team activities such as abseiling and flying fox. There will be land- and water-based expeditions such as

---

[3] Peter S. Goodman, "More wealth, more jobs, but not for everyone: What fuels the backlash on trade". *The New York Times*, 28 September 2016. https://www.nytimes.com/2016/09/29/business/economy/more-wealth-more-jobs-but-not-for-everyone-what-fuels-the-backlash-on-trade.html.

cycling, urban trekking, sailing and kayaking. And there will also be facilitated reflection sessions to foster self-discovery. These activities will build confidence, resilience and teamwork. And to be honest, when we first mooted this idea, we were aware of the values that it will bring. We were very convinced that it will be good for our young people, but we were also reminded quite quickly about the risks involved. What if a child falls? What if a child gets injured and so on? And that's where I think you can help us as well — believe in the core principles of why we are doing this and help us manage the risks. Part of this programme is to subject our children to some risk so that they can be resilient, so that they can be physically agile. So, risk is unavoidable; we will manage it as much as we can. But to do an OBS in a totally risk-free environment would be an oxymoron, and it's not something that we would encourage.

This five-day camp will give all our Singaporeans a shared experience, much like what watching the National Day Parade

OBS participants on a water raft they had constructed.
Source: The Straits Times © SPH Media Limited. Reprinted with permission.

rehearsals has been for our Primary 5 students, so that all Singaporean youths, after we have started this programme, can talk about their OBS experience. It is also important that our youth make friends with peers from different backgrounds. So, the camp will mix students across schools.

Beyond building bonds, we also provide pathways for our youth to develop and act on a sense of service. The Youth Corps provides a range of programmes from *ad hoc* community service events to regular volunteering programmes. Through these programmes, our youth can step up to become service leaders — from first being a participant in a project to becoming a coordinator, and eventually becoming a leader and mentor. The National Youth Council (NYC) also offers the Youth Expedition Project grant scheme that supports youth to embark on service-learning projects in the Association of Southeast Asian Nations (ASEAN), China, India and here in Singapore. NYC regularly organises platforms for youths to come together and ideate on co-creating a better Singapore. These sessions give them the chance to hear and understand different viewpoints from different Singaporeans so that they can come together to develop a common view of Singapore's future. Through these discussions, they find common reference points and ways of resolving differences. Where they can, they find mutual interests; where they cannot, they learn to compromise for a common good. This is important if we are going to be united and resilient as a country.

What the Singapore Children's Society has been doing for the community is very much aligned with this part of our narrative about building a caring society. I would urge you to also focus on creating more volunteering opportunities. We see the process of giving, in other words getting volunteers to step forward to give, as equally important a process in shaping the values of our young people, as the process of the needy segment receiving help. From MCCY's perspective, we are putting more emphasis on the segment that is giving, and we would like to have more opportunities for Singaporeans to give in a very hands-on and action-oriented way.

Conclusion

I have spoken about three mindsets and values that our youth need to have — an enterprising spirit and eagerness to dream, a curious mind and willingness to learn, and a sense of rootedness and community. Enterprise and curiosity will help our youth acquire the tools to succeed in the global marketplace. The sense of community will provide meaning to their endeavours. With these values, they will achieve their goal of living fulfilling lives in a caring and cohesive Singapore.

Instilling these values is a shared responsibility among all of us — the government, the youths themselves, their families and our society at large. My challenge to all of you working with youth and children is to create environments conducive to the development of these attributes. Promote creativity, an openness to risk and experimentation, a respect for lifelong learning and the strength to bounce back from adversity. Do more to expose our youth to the world and make them curious. And always remind them of their responsibilities to their fellow Singaporeans.

If we do this right, not only will our children and youth find their way in the world, they will also become the leaders of tomorrow.

CHAPTER THREE

Definition of Success — Doing Justice to One's Blessings

Chan Chun Sing

About the Speaker

As a parent of three, Mr Chan Chun Sing understands the aspirations that parents have for their children. But he also fervently believes that parents should acquire an appreciation for their children's strengths and weaknesses, and help them discover their own pathways. Having to figure things out for himself when he was young helped him to be an independent learner. With this in mind, he is of the view that parents should give their children room to grow and make their own decisions, while supporting and guiding them in their pursuits.

Instead of overemphasising performance in examinations, his hope is for parents to inspire a sense of curiosity in their children and instil in them a desire to learn. "It's not just about performance to meet some aspirations or standards, but it's really to find meaning in what you are doing and understand what you can do to help yourself and help others," asserts Mr Chan.

Mr Chan is the current Minister for Education and Minister-in-Charge of the Public Service. He was the Minister in the Prime Minister's Office (PMO) and Secretary-General of the National Trades Union Congress

(NTUC) when he delivered the lecture *Definition of Success — Doing Justice to One's Blessings*. This lecture, which was part of the 65th anniversary celebrations of the Singapore Children's Society, was followed by a public forum *Rethinking Success* where the audience discussed the impact of parents' expectations on children's aspirations.

A Singapore Armed Forces Overseas Scholar and President's Scholar who graduated with First Class Honours in Economics from Christ's College at the University of Cambridge, Mr Chan served in the army for more than two decades and was appointed Chief of Army prior to joining politics in 2011. He was elected as a Member of Parliament for the Group Representation Constituency of Tanjong Pagar at the start of his political career.

Mr Chan assiduously observed in his lecture that as a society, Singaporean parents tend to conceive of their children's success in fairly select ways, just like the hunter-gatherer society in the tale he narrated, where success was predetermined by the village elders. In comparison, Mr Chan's mother did not impose high expectations on him, and only asked that he not repeat any academic year. Being retained for a year would mean the family paying an extra year's worth of school fees; it would also mean a year's delay in being able to work and support the family.

Chan Chun Sing as a
Secondary 1 schoolboy.

Having exceeded his mother's expectations of him in school and university, he went on to assume various senior roles in government. In addition to being Minister in the PMO and Secretary-General of NTUC, he held ministerial positions at the Ministry of Trade and Industry, Ministry of Social and Family Development, Ministry of Defence and Ministry of Community Development, Youth and Sports. He was also the Minister of State for Information, Communications and the Arts.

The 65th Anniversary Conference Lecture, delivered 24 November 2017

Today, I will start off with a story. If there is a close resemblance to any particular society or individuals, it is purely coincidental.

Once upon a time, there lived a society where people made their living by hunting wild animals and engaging in agriculture. They were a contented society. One day, the elders of the society came together and wanted to know who, among the next generation, were the best and how to encourage them to do even better. They talked about it and said, "Why don't we give out some awards? We could give awards to those who are the best in our society." Everyone thought it was a wonderful idea. Then the natural question was how to determine who was the best? They thought about it and said, "Hmm, since we live in the valley, the ability to run and to run fast is the most important." Everyone agreed.

So, they held a competition annually and whoever ran the fastest was deemed the best. Within a few years, everyone was training to be faster. Many younger people were passing the test easily, so the elders felt that the yardstick they had previously set was no longer good enough and that they needed a new criterion to determine success. They thought about it and said, "Now, we must have a competition where participants must run fast and have good aim when shooting!" This is because they were also a hunter-gatherer society. True enough, once the criterion was announced, everyone started training to not only run faster but also shoot better.

This went on for a couple of years until the elders were dissatisfied again. Everyone was surpassing the standards in running and shooting. Once again, they had an elders' conference. They decided, "Not only must we run fast, we must also shoot straight, and get people to lift heavy weights." Lo and behold, once again everyone was training to be faster, improving their aim and becoming stronger.

Unfortunately, the sky opened up one day and heavy rain poured over the valley. The valley was flooded and remained this way for a long while. Fortunately, some members of the society had learnt to adapt to the circumstances and were able to swim, row a boat and fish. And because of that, the society was able to survive. After the flood subsided, the elders met again and said, "Hmm, the flood has taught us a lesson. Henceforth, our best will be those who know how to swim." From that year onwards, the competition focused on who could swim the fastest or the longest.

This continued until one day, the volcano nearby erupted. Fortunately for them, some people who could climb the cliffs had seen the eruption and the lava flowing down towards the valley. This group of climbers warned the community that perhaps it was time for them to seek higher ground.

Once things had gone back to normal, it was a very confusing time for the elders. Again, they asked themselves the question, "What should next year's competition be about?" This time they could not agree on the new criteria. Chaos ensued. Meanwhile, as the elders were disagreeing, the children were happily pursuing their own interests.

I will end here and let you imagine the rest of the story. I thought it would be useful to reflect upon this story and share three points before proceeding to the dialogue.

First, I think very often as adults, we would like to set the yardstick and measure our children's success, perhaps based on our own experience. Or we impose upon them expectations that we had for ourselves but did not manage to achieve. There is nothing wrong with having expectations *per se*. The question is whether success should be measured by a single yardstick.

Second, you may have realised that I have designed the story to show that in order for a society to be resilient, its people need diverse skill sets. Today, we may be a hunter-gatherer society. Tomorrow, we might face floods. And in the future, we might face a volcanic eruption. Indeed, we need a society with diverse skill sets to help us survive and overcome these challenges.

Lastly, we tend to focus very much on defining what success means for our children. Again, there is nothing wrong with that. However, if our measurement of success for our children starts to define all that they can achieve for themselves in their lifetime, then perhaps we have inevitably shaped them in a certain pre-conceived way, which may not be the most helpful.

One of the key learnings from the story I just shared is that the way the elders defined success for each generation of children might have had nothing to do with the children's individual aspirations.

In addition, there is a dimension of how they were able to collectively contribute to the success and survival of their society. We may have individual weaknesses or be inadequate in some ways, but collectively, each of us can play a part in creating the diversity that strengthens the resilience of our country. Our definition of success should be focused not just on what we can achieve for ourselves but also on what we can achieve for our broader community.

Question: My twin sons are currently sitting for their A-Level (Singapore-Cambridge General Certificate of Education Advanced Level) exams. The problem is they don't know what they want to do. They have been offered various government scholarships and early admissions by some local universities. Would you be able to give some advice? I know you studied Economics in Cambridge. How did you choose your path?

Answer: The world is quite different from the time when I completed my A-Levels. I probably wouldn't have been able to finish my A-Levels if not for the series of bursaries and scholarships that I obtained from primary school all the way up to junior college. Life was quite straightforward, we did not have so many choices. If you passed your exams, you would go to the next level. If you did not, you would probably have to find a job.

But that narrative has changed. In my experience, human beings are motivated by two sets of forces. The first set of forces has to do with hunger and fear. I think for my generation, that would probably have been the predominant set of forces that drove us. The second set of forces that tends to drive people to excel has to do with passion. The current generation, as compared to the past, is driven more so by passion than fear. They are like the Bill Gates of the world, I want to do it because I want to change the world to be a better place. So, we will have to help the younger generation understand both sets of forces, but let them decide for themselves what motivates them more — hunger and fear or passion.

When I finished my A-Levels, the choice was either to get a scholarship and continue my studies or find a job. A scholarship was not a means to Cambridge for me. A scholarship actually meant securing a job and a way to bring home the bacon. When I applied for the government scholarship, I wanted to be a librarian. In the past, the National Library at Stamford Road was the only place that I could read books for free, and I thought that being a librarian meant they were going to pay me to read books, which sounded like a good job.

However, there was no Librarian category when I applied, so I selected the *Open Merit Scholarship*, which meant I could be deployed to various government agencies, including the National Library Board. My second choice was between the Legal Service and the Singapore Armed Forces (SAF), and I decided to give the latter a try.

When I was called up for the interview, they asked if I wanted to join the SAF. I asked them if they were sure — I almost failed my Basic Military Training and also almost failed my shooting test. In the end, I was still sent to the SAF. My mother asked me then, "Why did you take up the SAF Scholarship?" And I said, "I don't know. They offered me a job and I took it." So, she thought about it and said, "Oh, okay." Since I come from a single-parent family, we were not that well off financially; getting a job was most certainly better than not having one.

As I was not myopic, the SAF thought the Air Force would suit me well. I joined the Air Force Cadets for two weeks. However, my mother was concerned and told me in Mandarin to be 脚踏实地 — that I should keep my feet firmly on the ground. I decided to join the army instead. But which part of the army? They said, "Infantry." So, that is how I ended up in the Infantry.

Why I am sharing this anecdote is because, in life, one just never knows. Sometimes we are able to plan, but other times, you take things as they come. When I was in the Infantry, I had the privilege of meeting people from all walks of life. Being in the army taught me about life. It taught me that life was not just about where I wanted to go and what I wanted to seek. It was also about how I could contribute.

For some of the soldiers that I commanded, joining the SAF during National Service was challenging because they could not earn a living for their families since they were only paid an allowance. That's why I began asking myself what I could do for them. My promise to them was, "The only thing I can do for you is that when you walk out of the gates after two years of National Service, you will not look down on yourself. And because you don't look down on yourself, nobody will look down on you." When I became a battalion commander, I was extremely proud when my men, regardless of their background, banded together to complete the half marathon as a unit in cadence. They took care of one another.

Question: You mentioned about the need to have diverse skill sets as a society. But my sense is that many parents would read that as an individual child needing to have diverse skill sets, which probably explains why many children attend enrichment classes and so on. So then, is it better for children's well-being to go back to basics? What kind of advice would you give to parents?

Answer: Let's ask ourselves as parents, as educators, what's our most important role for our children? If you can only choose one role, one mission, one promise that you would give to your child, what would that promise be? Is it to help them to excel? Or is it something else? Anybody wants to try?

Audience member 1: A happy, meaningful life.

Audience member 2: I will love you unconditionally.

Audience member 3: Encourage you wherever you are.

Audience member 4: To be the best you can be.

Audience member 5: Support is always there.

Answer (contd.): Support is always there. So, be what you want to be, and the support is there. Unconditional love. How about this? We can help each child appreciate his or her own unique gifts and, collectively as a society, remain diverse. I think it will be too much to ask our children to have a myriad of skill sets. Realistically, there is only a certain level of diversity in terms of the skill sets that one can have. I'm not gifted in sports nor the arts, but I have to find my own gift and, in hoping that I find my own gift, realise that I can use this gift to be a blessing to others.

Question: For several years, the government has indicated that the education system will change to be less grades-focused, but I see my kids in primary school doing maths questions that I used to do in secondary school. My sister-in-law tells me that my nieces, who are in Primary 3, are learning Chinese words that she learnt in secondary school as well. So, my question is how and when will the education system really change from being focused on grades?

Answer: I don't like to use the word "system" in my life because, think about it, who is the system? Who makes up the system? We are all collectively responsible; we all can make individual choices for ourselves, our families and our children. We all have a responsibility to do this together. Remember the story of the elders? We choose to be the kind of elders we want to be.

Let me share an example. A parent told me her child was not given full marks for a question because he did not give the stock answer. I was most interested in how the parent reacted to the child. I asked her if she was happy with her child's answer, and she said she was because his answer was creative. Indeed, just because our children do not give the stock answer to an open-ended question, do we make our children feel that they are unworthy or that they are any less because they did not score that A? This is something we should reflect on — because how we respond will set the tone for how our child will respond in future, and the cycle continues.

My appeal to all parents is this — even if your child does not come home with an A-grade, please do not deflate the child's self-confidence by making him or her feel that he or she is unworthy. The impact will be a lasting one for the child. It will perpetuate the misconception that if you don't meet that single yardstick of success, you are unworthy. This would not only impact the child but also many more generations to come.

Personally, I did not do well in both Art and Music in kindergarten. My mother, of course, asked me why I failed, but she also accepted that I am just not gifted in those areas. However, I did quite well in Mathematics, so I focused on that. We all have our shortfalls in life, but that should not be the end of the world, so let us not make it the end of the world for our children. Let us help our children realise their gifts and enable them to use their gifts to bless others.

Question: I was just reflecting on your story earlier about having diverse skill sets so that as a society we can remain resilient throughout all the challenges. I also firmly believe that every one of us present here fully buys into the idea that there's more than one definition of success and we are all working very hard every day to support our children in taking ownership of their own successes.

However, I was also thinking about the whole idea of the swimmers, the climbers and the runners. They have always existed in the society. Just that we were not able to recognise them for their strengths, and therefore, we did not think that they were the best. I was also thinking about how success is not just about passing or failing, and thinking about whether the system is ready to acknowledge our kids and their different strengths and interests.

So, how can we as parents, as aunts and uncles, as brothers and sisters, even as social service organisations which work with kids every day, how then can we encourage them not just to recognise what their gift is but also to identify what they can use their gifts for? If my gift is not recognised in the society as a strength, does it then mean I'm a failure? How can we as a society nurture a culture of helping kids to see what they can use their gifts for and then take ownership and achieve success in their own right? What can we do and where can we start?

Answer: We all like to seek recognition from the people around us. That's human nature. As a result of this, we tend to feel very uncertain when we do not receive external affirmation. There is no easy way to overcome this. On one hand, we need to be confident that what we do is meaningful for ourselves and for the society. Yet, on the other hand, we need to affirm the diverse talents that our people have on a societal level.

In order to achieve this, we need to help our people feel valued and confident. Once our people feel valued, they can then share their gifts with the rest. Due to certain circumstances in life, not everyone has the same starting point. However, perhaps it is enough that we do the best that we can and as a society encourage people to realise their gifts and use their gifts for others.

As I mentioned earlier, I worked with people from various backgrounds during my time in the army. Each of them had a valuable gift to offer. Some were very loyal, and I could trust them with my life if we went into battle. Others taught me determination and the strength to pick ourselves up after failure. I learnt something from all of them. In fact, in life, anyone can be our mentor and teach us something valuable. I would be frank that in my days in the military, the three people who have taught me the most in life, none of them was a graduate.

None of these people is someone who we would usually associate with being a mentor, but they were gifted people in their own ways. In the short time that I had the privilege of serving with them, I found that I could always learn something from them, such as loyalty, camaraderie and taking care of family.

As a round-up, I hope that you can take away these three main points. First, while we all aspire for excellence, excellence does not have to just reside in one dimension. Second, diversity adds to our resilience as a society. We may not be individually diverse, but we can be collectively diverse. Last, but not the least, I hope that our definition of success for ourselves and our children is not limited to what we can get and achieve for ourselves, but for society as well.

CHAPTER FOUR

Growing Up
in an Unequal Society

Teo You Yenn

About the Speaker

Inequality is a topic that is salient and significant to Associate Professor Teo You Yenn because of its profound consequences on people's lives and well-being. A/P Teo argues that people have "different chances in life if they differ in their ability to access things that they need". This ties in with recent research she has conducted. In a local study focused on defining the minimum standards of living and the financial costs involved in meeting basic needs,[1] she and her collaborators found that parents regularly prioritise their children's needs, particularly education needs as their children get older. Basic standards of living include not only food, clothing and shelter but also a sense of dignity, a sense of belonging, access to education, access to work-life balance and access to choices to participate in social, religious and cultural activities. Basic needs are context-specific and historically specific.

Currently a Provost's Chair in Sociology at Nanyang Technological University, A/P Teo received her Doctorate of Philosophy in Sociology

---

[1] Ng Kok Hoe, Teo You Yenn, Neo Yu Wei, Ad Maulod, Stephanie Chok & Wong Yee Lok (2021). *What People Need in Singapore: A Household Budgets Study*. https://whatsenough.sg/key-findings-mis2021/

from the University of California, Berkeley, and has been teaching undergraduates since 1998. Her research focuses on poverty, inequality, governance and state-society dynamics, gender and class.

The author of two books, *This Is What Inequality Looks Like*[2] and *Neoliberal Morality in Singapore: How Family Policies Make State and Society,*[3] as well as numerous journal articles and book chapters, A/P Teo has, over the last decade, contributed regularly to public debate through public lectures and written commentaries in the local newspapers and media. She is also one of the founding editors of Academia.SG, a platform set up in 2019 to promote Singapore studies and encourage critical debate about the state of intellectual life in Singapore.

Her previous work on family and pronatalist policies, where she examined how people negotiate housing and childcare policies, led her to observe that there were strong and constraining norms around what it means to be an ideal Singaporean. She came to conclude that public policy plays an important role in generating people's habits and practices. She began to question what this means for people who do not and cannot easily fit that ideal. This further led her to think about the welfare regime in Singapore and to appraise how public goods are designed and delivered in the local context. Her observations of families in public rental housing piqued her interest in better understanding the challenges faced by low-income families. That led to three years of ethnographic research, from which she shared two themes, one on schooling and education, and the other on youths, in her lecture, *Growing Up in an Unequal Society*.

In reflecting also on the minimum income standards study mentioned earlier, A/P Teo points out that there is "zero controversy" across society about the fact that tuition is a basic need, although there is a certain ambivalence among parents. Parents wish that tuition classes

---

[2] Teo You Yenn, *This Is What Inequality Looks Like* (Singapore: Ethos Books, 2018).
[3] Teo You Yenn, *Neoliberal Morality in Singapore: How Family Policies Make State and Society* (London and New York: Routledge, 2011).

were not a necessity and that their children were not under as much pressure from the education system.

Teo You Yenn in 1977.

Given that many children from lower-income households "fall behind almost immediately as they enter the first year of compulsory schooling", as A/P Teo mentions in her lecture, it is not incomprehensible that these children need the same help that other children from higher-income families are receiving from their tuition teachers. A/P Teo notes that the parents of these other children are being rational in wanting to ensure that their children do not fall behind. The shadow education industry exists because there is a need for it. She points out that parents are ultimately very concerned about future employment prospects and their children's capacity to earn decent wages. Educational outcomes are closely tied to wages, which in turn determine our access to basic needs such as housing, healthcare and education. She makes a good point: organising and distributing a public good as important as education in more equitable ways would pave the way for different practices, leading to myriad different outcomes.

The 12th Lecture, delivered 15 September 2018[4]

A Moment of Possibility

So, you may have heard, I wrote a book. In writing this talk, I had to make sure that someone who hasn't read the book could still get something out of it. There is quite a lot in what I'll say today that will be familiar to those of you who have read it. Those of you who have not read it, I hope you will still do so after today. There is a lot I cover in the book that is difficult to convey in a lecture.

Last year, when I was writing this book, I basically lived inside it. I would occasionally come out to carry out other responsibilities in life, but for most of last year, I was entirely immersed in writing. By the end of 2017, when the manuscript was going into production, I was pretty exhausted. And I thought, in 2018, I'm going to relax a little, catch my breath, catch up on sleep, and start paying attention to my family and my friends again.

My plan for resting in 2018 has so far not worked out. This book has taken on a life of its own. And I've spent a lot of the past eight months giving talks, meeting with people, writing further commentaries and reflecting on the various responses to the book.

I mention this because the response to the book strikes me as evidence that we are in a moment of possibility. I've been tremendously encouraged over the past months to see that there is such great concern for the issues of poverty and inequality. And I have also been very impressed and heartened, judging both from what people write to me and also what they ask me at talks, that there is much desire to want to do something to reduce both poverty and inequality. I wrote the book because I had a vague hunch that these things are true, but the reach of this book and the significant responses it has provoked has exceeded my expectations. I am glad ultimately that my plans for rest this year have not worked out.

---

[4] An animated, abridged version of this lecture can be viewed at: https://www.youtube.com/watch?v=N9G5nKnpTWA&t=146s

I start by making this point — that we are in a moment of possibility — because I think it is important to recognise.

It is important to recognise for two reasons: first, as individuals, we live in our own lives, and it is not always obvious that there is a collective that shares some of our values and some of our aspirations. I have made this argument in my work over many years — that our lives are very individualised. As Singaporeans, we hold this stereotype of ourselves as apathetic and disengaged. And this can feel very lonely. I think that loneliness, that lack of sense of solidarity with others, and that sense that other people don't care, can be very disempowering. And it can lead us to be static, to feel that we ourselves are unable to take initiative and act.

So I start with the responses I've received about my book to highlight that a lot of Singaporeans do in fact care. Of course, it is not everyone, nor a majority, but it is nonetheless significant and meaningful. And I think all of us should recognise and be encouraged by this.

Second, it is important to recognise this as a moment of possibility because a moment of possibility is just that — moment, possibility. It may be fleeting, it is potential not yet translated into reality, and what happens in the next years depends on what we all do with it. I do not take for granted that this moment will lead to real reduction in poverty, real changes to how our opportunity structures work, real improvements in redistributing our country's ample resources and real improvements in our society's inequality problems. What happens to this potential depends on what we do in the next five, ten, 20 years.

I expect that many of you are here because you have in one way or another also been on this journey, paying attention to or participating in discussions about poverty and inequality in Singapore in recent years. I think the book has gotten the reception it has because the issues I speak of in the book have been on many of our minds over the last few years. Perhaps you have read the book and shared it with others. Or others have shared it with you. Given the size of this audience, I must presume you come from quite a wide variety of fields. It will be impossible to speak directly to solutions that fit perfectly your needs. I hope what you get out of today are questions to think about as well as principles to think with. And I hope you will be able to adapt and apply them to the situations you face and are trying to work through.

I will return to the question of possibilities, and to limitations, at the end of my lecture. But now, let me turn more directly to the subject of today's talk — growing up in an unequal society.

Ethnography: Childhood and Education — My Findings Found Me

My book is based on three years of ethnographic research. I wanted, broadly speaking, to study the everyday lives of people in Singapore who live with low income. I focused my work mostly on families with children living in Housing & Development Board (HDB) rental flats.

One principle underlying ethnographic research is that there has to be a certain openness when you approach the topic of study. You approach in an open-ended way, spending time in a place, having many informal conversations, without very rigid survey or interview questions. Through this approach, you can learn things you did not know to ask about. You can gather data that disturbs pre-existing notions and biases, that expands the view of what's relevant in a context.

The framing of questions can already limit what you can and cannot see. This is especially so on a topic on which limited work has been done, and on a population which is marginalised and stigmatised in some way. The ethnographic approach that I took allowed me to see, hear and learn many things I could not have thought to ask before I began the work. It was a research strategy that ultimately allowed a glimpse of the complexity of people's lives.

Children playing along the common corridors of a HDB rental block.
Source: The Straits Times © SPH Media Limited. Reprinted with permission.

The first thing to note about my research findings is that I ended up finding out a lot about family lives and family dynamics because this is what people talked about, because this is what preoccupies them. But an important specificity to add to that is that family lives are bound up with other aspects of life, and, in particular, with work — employment. So, I spend significant time in my book discussing the links between family life and employment.

A further thing to add is that family life, in households where there are young people, revolves around and centres on children's needs. I was not specifically looking to study education or childhood issues in my research. The difficulties with education and the difficulties parents face in raising youth — these topics found me. I did not go in search of them. They emerged naturally in conversation, and they emerged repeatedly in conversation. They were a source of much concern and great anxiety for parents.

That I didn't go chasing after these issues, and that they emerged, is itself a finding. It reveals the centrality of kids in parents' lives, and it reveals the place formal education plays as a key source of anxiety.

Growing Up Unequal: Context Matters

Two essays in my book deal particularly with the lives and well-being of children. One zooms in on the question of schooling and education, while the other looks more broadly at youth.

In both, this is the main point I'd like you to keep in mind: context matters. I'll explain as I go along what I mean by that and why it's crucial.

Education/Schooling: "I Want My Children Better Than Me"

In my conversations with parents, education came up repeatedly as a major source of anxiety. Low-income parents — and especially mothers — told me that an important reason why they quit their jobs or cut back on wage work is that their kids were struggling in school. They talked about children failing weekly spelling tests or teachers calling them up regularly to speak to them about their kids' problems with schoolwork.

Many of the kids fall behind almost immediately as they enter the first year of compulsory schooling.[5] They are less advanced than kids from wealthier families, who can read and write by the day they enter Primary 1. Very quickly, many barely pass or com-

---

[5] In Singapore, under the Compulsory Education Act (2000), children must attend primary school from the year they turn seven, unless an exemption is granted.

pletely fail English and Mathematics. They usually still do reasonably well in Mother Tongue, which many use at home, signalling that the kids generally do have the capacity to learn when there is sufficient exposure to a subject. In Primary 1 and 2, many of the kids from low-income families are identified as having problems and pulled out of class for extra coaching. While this can help, it is not easy for the kids to catch up, since the more advanced kids continue to move forward at a fast pace. By Primary 3, many kids from low-income families are tracked and banded into lower-performing classes.

Although schools vary in how obvious the banding is at Primary 3 and 4, kids themselves are well aware of where they stand *vis-à-vis* others. By Primary 5 and 6, many of the kids do so poorly that they have to switch to what is known as Foundation level[6] for some or all of their subjects. While most parents I spoke with reported their kids still go to school regularly, it is apparent that many develop a sense of themselves as inferior to others and start to feel quite demoralised. In some cases, kids begin to resist going to school. If conditions are unstable at home, parents also find it difficult to manage their children's school schedules. If they do indeed stop going to school regularly, their social connections at school will suffer. When they return, the absence of friends, teasing or bullying from schoolmates, can make staying the course difficult.

How should we interpret all this? As I've said, context matters.

Both children and their parents face many difficulties due to complex home situations that have little to do with schools, but the schooling experience itself is crucial for understanding their relative lack of educational success. This becomes especially clear when speaking with parents who are, despite all their challenges, getting their kids to go to school every day.

---

[6] The curriculum of a subject taken at Foundation level is a subset of that at Standard level.

The Singapore education system is one that demands precocity. This means that it demands children to be able to display their skills at early ages, and displaying certain qualities in reading and mathematics early brings rewards. How does the demand for precocity play out in generating and perpetuating inequalities?

People who work with kids will know that students are sensitive about how they are compared to their peers. A teacher I spoke with told me that students who are in lower bands say things like "I stupid lah" or "I lazy what". They do not try because they do not believe they can possibly succeed. Teachers working with kids in low tracks have to spend time and energy on behavioural issues linked to low self-esteem and lack of motivation. Children are more disruptive in classrooms and are more likely to skip school or neglect homework. This phenomenon is not something limited to Singapore nor unknown to pedagogical researchers.

Jeannie Oakes, in a classic study on tracking,[7] shows that one of the detrimental effects of tracking students according to narrow criteria of academic abilities is that students in low tracks often think of themselves as poor learners and thus do not try as hard as students in high tracks who think of themselves as capable. In other words, low motivation, a reason cited by educators who work with kids from low-income families, is something reproduced within the school context. Specifically, the sorting and labelling of kids is something of a self-fulfilling prophecy that shapes learning behaviours.

There are some positive things to an education system that has multiple tracks. Kids are not completely thrown out. There are still tracks open to them, which prevent them from dropping out of school altogether. At the same time, however, there also

---

[7] Jeannie Oakes, *Keeping Track: How Schools Structure Inequality* (New Haven: Yale University Press, 1985).

appears an irrational outcome: most of these kids appear to be of regular intelligence and do not have learning disabilities, but they are labelled slow from a young age. In speaking to an Allied Educator whose job is to work with kids with learning disabilities, I learnt that it takes some time for her to figure out which kids have disabilities. Why? Because most of the kids who come to her attention are behind simply because they have not had as much exposure to school materials and not because they are unable to learn in neurotypical ways. In other words, given time and exposure, they are no less capable of learning than most other children. They lack exposure for a variety of reasons: they have less preschool education; their parents do not speak English (or the type of English required in schools); there is limited reading at home, and they do not have extra coaching by tuition teachers. In other words, the main reason they fall behind can be traced to their relative class disadvantages.

Question: Do you think making preschool education compulsory and paid for by the government will help children from poorer socioeconomic backgrounds do better in school?

Answer: I think that support for parents with young children is extremely important so that parents can do what they need to do, whether it's wage work, housework or whatever kind of labour they need to do. Support for child-rearing ought to be universally accessible and affordable to all, and the quality in that area should be good across the board rather than very uneven.

In that way, I think it is important, certainly, to make sure that all parents, regardless of their economic backgrounds, have good access to some form of childcare support and that children have good access to good quality childcare regardless of their parents' income.

Now, having said that, the framing of the question is very specific — whether to make preschool education compulsory, and I should comment on that framing. So, the question is whether I think the Compulsory Education Act should be brought forward to cover kids of lower ages. I think this is something we have to be careful about, particularly if nothing changes in the primary school system. Because what is very likely to happen, if you *only* do that, is you bring forward the competition; you bring forward the intensification of the education arms race. I don't think that *that* is a step in the right direction.

Question: You express reservations about banding and I'm with you on the view that it would impact those who are *slower* learners. But what is the solution that you have in mind? If we don't have banding or streaming, would we be holding back those who are able to perform better, those who are early starters?

Answer: I think that I'm not against some form of specialisation at some point during education, but what we have is actually a system where kids are very early, already separated into different groups. Child development is such that in the early years there's a lot of variation, which then means that it's not good to try to predict where children are going to end up by looking very early for certain kinds of qualities. A child who's able to read at 5, versus a child who's able to read at 7, versus a child who's able to read at 9 — all things equal, meaning if they really have equal opportunities later on, I don't think those kids are going to end up being very different contributors in society. All those three kids ultimately are going to be able to read and they're going to be able to also cultivate lots of other skills.

When you have a kid who is not ready yet to walk, you wouldn't force them and say *you must walk now*, but essentially, with reading and writing, we're doing that at a pretty early age when we know that, developmentally, children are at different places and that that is not a good point to predict how they will do in the long run, given more time.

About the more tricky question, about whether this holds kids back — again, this goes back to two things. One is the extent to which we think children can only learn in environments where other children are exactly like them, and I don't think that that's the case. Children can, in fact, learn in mixed environments and there are specific pedagogies actually directed at getting children who are quite different to learn in the same space. Again, the fundamental belief there is that people have varied strengths. Right now I think one of our fundamental beliefs is that only some people have strengths. But if our fundamental belief is that people have varied strengths and everyone has strengths, then we won't think of it as holding some children back because those children who can read and write early, there are some things they can't do that they can learn from the kids who are not reading and writing early, and those kids have other strengths, maybe in sports or the arts.

I think it is possible as human beings to have multiple strengths. But we have to give that time and we have to allow kids to not feel that only certain kinds of strengths are valuable and that other kinds of strengths are useless.

Turn our view around and we see that, given the ubiquity of enrichment centres and tutors, some kids — because of class advantages — are advantaged in a system where early exposure and precocity are rewarded. The kids who are able to run forward the moment the gates are open are neither more meritorious nor more deserving.

Why do I call this an irrational outcome? If we think of schools as places of learning, if equality of opportunity is upheld as our education system's mantra, and if the purpose of mass education is to train as many capable individuals as we can who will grow up to be contributing members of our society, then kids who have insufficient exposure outside of school should have sufficient exposure within it and sufficient time to even out the advantages or disadvantages resulting from class differences. They should not be punished for having insufficient exposure outside of it. In rewarding precocity — expecting kids to be able to read and write when they begin Primary 1, for example — we are rewarding qualities that are acquired outside of school and in the process losing valuable potential of talents and strengths in kids who need time and exposure.

The effects of early sorting and labelling are profound for parents as well as kids. Parents with more money also tend to be parents who have the confidence to say: my kid is not stupid, he or she just needs more help. How our kids are branded by schools, the information parents get from schools about how they compare vis-à-vis other children — these shape our ideas about our own children and what they are capable of. If I believe my child is fundamentally, even with bad grades, capable, then my solution is to find help, especially if I have money to pay for this help. If, in contrast, over time, I am told repeatedly by teachers that my child is very weak or unmotivated, my sense of my kid is that she or he is like me, not so good in school, not likely to do well. If I do not have money for tutors anyway, then my aspirations for my child too will be adjusted accordingly.

Parents' opinions and actions feed into a child's sense of themselves and their potential. Many of the parents I meet have high hopes that their children will do better than them, that they won't end up with such hard lives, but they parent in a context where their children are already branded as weaker, as lesser, as not as smart and not as capable. It is incredibly difficult to transcend that and to see their kids as still having talents and value. I see many low-income parents trying to do this, but like many of us who try our best to form independent opinions, we are not immune to the voices of others. We parent in specific social contexts and those contexts shape our hopes, our aspirations and our actions. We depend strongly on teachers' assessments and understandings of our children. We evaluate our children according to what seems *normal* in our society.

For many low-income parents I speak with, a sense of resignation sets in. An acceptance of a child's poor results and lacks come to define the dynamics within the family. In many of the stories families tell themselves about themselves, children are good at soccer, or dancing, or cooking, or helping with housework and care, but hopeless at Mathematics and English. Once solidified into common sense, both parents and children have a hard time coming out from under these labels.

The home environment of low-income kids is indeed not always conducive to studying. Spaces are small, family relationships are sometimes tense and material hardships are persistent. But this could be said to be the case for many Singaporean adults who now find themselves middle-class in contemporary Singapore. Many of my peers grew up in exactly these *not conducive* environments. This perhaps explains higher-income Singaporeans' reluctance to interrogate systemic inequality and an attendant rush to judge the low-income: if I could overcome hardship, why can't they?

To understand the persistence of low educational achievement and what appears to be the reproduction of class inequalities among the low-income today, we must look beyond individual families' practices. We have to examine the broader social context and important developments in the education system's criteria, dynamics and principles. Importantly, although counter-intuitive, we have to look at wider social practices of parents across class lines. In the 1980s, when I was in primary school, I did not have tuition, and none of my friends did. My parents spent approximately zero hours a week helping me with my homework, roughly the same amount of time my classmates' parents spent on theirs. It is very important, when those who are now wealthier than they were growing up declare that they were able to over-come, to remember that we are not living in the 1970s or the 1980s Singapore anymore.

So what is today's context? Across class lines, I am struck by the amount of time and energy parents today — regardless of income and profession — put in to keeping an eye on their children's progress in school. The difficulty of the curriculum, the understanding that exams have high-stake consequences for their kids' futures, and the difficulty of teaching one's own children have fuelled the growth of the tuition industry. Parents with ample means use these to help their children from the get-go (in some cases as young as preschool) and on a regular basis (i.e., throughout the school years). Parents with moderate means forgo other household needs and hire tutors in crucial exam years and/or on subjects especially tough for their kids. Tuition has become a billion-dollar industry, with parents spending significant proportions of household income on it.

Quite apart from tuition for academic subjects, an industry also exists for enrichment programmes. Some of these are meant to further hone skills that contribute to academic performance in schools. Others are essentially insurance policies — ways for kids to develop other types of *talents* that can also open doors to *good schools* or higher tracks in case their academic results fall short. That these exist also tell us an additional thing: some parents are diligently learning about how the system works and are active campaigners on behalf of their children.

I do not fault parents for wanting the best for their children, but we must acknowledge that this type of campaigning is not class-neutral: it comes more easily to people who have themselves succeeded in the system and understand its logic, who feel a sense of entitlement in their interactions with teachers, who have time to devote to this labour, and who have budgets that allow for various aspects of this, including for buying books, hiring tutors and cutting back on full-time employment.

Worries about inequalities in the education system often centre on the *low-performing* and focus on *levelling up*. Kids from low-income families are often the target group. The presence of numerous programmes, personnel and public expenditure intended to level up these kids, combined with the persistence of low performance among them, lead to the perception that kids from low-income families are less motivated or lack the right home environment for studying. More generally, many Singaporeans take for granted that the system is merit-based and that there are ample opportunities for everyone regardless of their family backgrounds.

These perspectives are not wrong *per se*, but they are insufficiently precise. In their imprecision, they slip into faulting low-income parents for the poor academic performance of their kids. The logic goes that if our systems are fair, then, surely, they fail because parents are not doing what they should be doing.

To understand why kids from low-income households do poorly in school, we would do well to understand what their lives at home are like. But we must also step back and situate their lives within the broader social context. This includes trying to understand what material conditions are like for parents, what school experiences are like for kids, and finally and least often done, what higher-income families are doing for their kids. It is when we do all these that we can have a more complete and accurate understanding of how kids from low-income families, within this system, are compelled to play a game they cannot win because someone else is setting the rules.

There is a lot of, and increasing, attention on the educational opportunities of kids from lower-income families. This is important. But if attention is only focused on this, in ten years, we will find ourselves standing more or less in the same spot.

We must frame the challenge differently — not as one where the problem is with the kids from low-income families, but where the problem is about our system of rewards as well as what parents from higher-income families are doing in response to this system of rewards. I know this is a very uncomfortable way of approaching the problem because it requires those of us who tend to be the ones talking about the problem to admit to our own complicity. But I think it is crucial if we are serious about this problem. We cannot keep doing the same things and expect the outcomes to be different.

Question: How would you convince parents from higher-income classes, *tiger mothers*, for example, to change a system which actually benefits them and, more importantly, benefits their children?

Answer: I focus so much on talking about structural and policy change because, in my work in the past, I see that that oftentimes we think it is beliefs and values that drive practices, but as a sociologist I often see evidence in the other direction — that it is practices that drive beliefs. In reality, it is probably a bit of back and forth.

Why do I emphasise this? In my earlier work when I looked at these so-called pro-family and pronatalist policies, I looked at how we have in Singapore created very strong beliefs and values about what being Singaporean is about, and that many of these strong norms are around applying for a HDB flat, going to the Registry of Marriages, getting the keys to your flat, having your ceremonial wedding, renovating your flat and then moving into your flat.

I delineate that because those things have become very strong Singaporean customs. We think of those strongly as the *normal* way to be Singaporean. But the *normal* way to be Singaporean has come about precisely because the policies that exist require people to behave in those ways in order to access public housing. So, a lot of those habits have come about precisely because the policy regime has shaped marriage practices in that way. What does that mean? It means practices shape beliefs and values. Rather than we believe marriage should look this way and therefore the policies responded to us and created those steps for us.

Of course, it is important to try to get people to think reflexively about their practices but, as I've said, people respond to the possibilities and constraints in their social context, and the possibilities and constraints have to change before people can be motivated to change their practices.

I don't think it is necessary to convince everyone to behave or to think in certain ways first before we change our practices. In order to convince parents from higher-income classes, what I have tried to do is precisely to try to show that indeed we all have a lot to gain from a system that is more equal. I think we all have a lot to gain if we live in a society where everybody's dignity and everybody's worth are respected and are inherent.

Youth: Growing Up Without Class Protections

Let me turn now to another set of findings — that of parenting youth. The essay from which this is drawn is titled *Growing Up Without Class Protections*.

It took me some time to see the form of this essay. This is because it took me a while to fully recognise that maintaining family relationships and maintaining authority over teenage kids is something that requires economic and social resources.

We often refer to family life as priceless or something we cannot put a price on. We imply that this is an area of life that cannot be bought, that somehow transcends money. I would like to highlight that while it is true that family life cannot be bought, certain material preconditions are nonetheless important. These preconditions do require money and what money is able to purchase.

Parenting is hard. And it is hard at multiple stages of life. It is hard in good circumstances, but harder yet when one has limited money, time and social standing.

When I speak to parents with teenage kids, these are the worries I hear of — kids who spend long hours away from home, hanging out with friends, kids who are unsure of their future vocations and who are struggling in school or dropping out, kids at risk of unplanned pregnancies, kids who have material needs that are not easily fulfilled and kids getting into trouble with the police for things like underage smoking, drugs and theft.

We often refer to at-risk youth or juvenile delinquents as if they automatically arise from bad neighbourhoods or dysfunctional families. The unspoken presumption is that youths go astray because parents are neglectful.

In the neighbourhoods where I did my research, it was often parents themselves who were expressing worries about their kids. I saw parents stressed out at their relationships with their teenage children, anxious about the fact that their kids were not listening to them, not coming home and not heeding their advice to take their parents' lives as cautionary tales. Clearly, the full story goes beyond one of parental neglect. After hearing parents express their worries and anxieties about kids, observing youths who hang out in low-income neighbourhoods and talking to social workers who work with young people, it strikes me that we don't adequately acknowledge the complex care needs (and care gaps) of youth. For our constant talk about family as the central unit of Singapore society, we pay very little attention to the everyday contours of family life.

When we begin to think about what youths need, we start to realise that parents in low-income households have a far more difficult time maintaining parental authority and that kids in low-income households do not have some of the protections that kids in higher-income households have.

When it comes to raising older kids, all parents struggle with maintaining some sphere of influence and authority. These are difficult because older kids are not like younger ones: they are able to go about their own everyday lives more independently than young children, and they are more aware of the world beyond their families. These two things are exactly the reasons lower-income parents struggle more than their higher-income counterparts.

In the essay, I describe the relevance of things we do not often talk about and which turn out are important for parenting youth: space, activities, pocket money, time, leisure, memories and the social standing of parents. In the interest of time, I'll just elaborate on the first today.

The reality of living in a low-income household is that there is little space for privacy. Even parents do not usually have a bedroom to themselves, so children certainly do not have much private space. When I visited homes, I saw people creatively use bed sheets and furniture to create partitions for some semblance of privacy for teenage children, especially girls. Still, the limitations of small flats mean that teenagers often find it more pleasant to spend time out of the home with friends than to be at home. In cases where relationships are fraught, as they often are between parents and teenage children regardless of class circumstances, this tendency to stay away naturally intensifies. When parents speak about wishing they could have bigger flats, one of the reasons they mention is that their kids can then have their own private space and perhaps even bring friends home to do homework, study and socialise, without being disturbed by younger siblings and other family members.

Unlike kids whose parents have money for enrichment and/or leisure activities, kids from low-income families have more hours in the day when they are unoccupied and away from adults. Compared to kids who are more financially dependent on their parents and therefore perhaps compelled to be more pliant, teenagers from low-income households more often earn their own pocket money through part-time work. In certain ways, they are more mature, independent and autonomous than their middle-class counterparts. They also tend to have peers who are similarly independent and therefore available to hang out with. As a result of this confluence of factors, parents are more likely to have limited influence over their kids. Kids sometimes stop going to school, stay out late, or stay away from home altogether. To put this plainly, middle-class parents hold sway over their teenage children partly through circumstance. Their financial dependence on parents, their use of personal spaces in their homes, and their scheduled activities are all conditions that grant parents continued access to influence over their everyday lives. Due to the absence of these conditions, authority is tough to maintain for low-income parents.

Context Matters: We Make Meaning, Decisions, Practices in Specific Social Conditions

Parenting is a socially embedded activity. By this, I mean two things. First, it is linked to other elements of everyday life — employment, leisure and schooling. Second, it is shaped by and rooted in the broader expectations, demands and habits of society. No one, in other words, is *just* a parent, and no one parents in isolation. While we are parents, we are also simultaneously employees, co-workers, spouses, siblings, daughters or sons, neighbours or friends. We figure out how to be parents partly from how teachers relate to us, what extended family members ask of us, what friends and acquaintances advise us, and what professionals — doctors, counsellors and social workers — tell us. Many of us like to imagine we are independent. People often declare, "I just do what I want to do and I don't care what other people say". But the reality is that what makes for a *good* or *bad* parent is shaped by circumstances and informed by criteria beyond any given individual's control.

Parenting under poor conditions involves high pressures from lack of money and lack of control over time. These lead to care gaps not only for very young children but also for older ones. They make building family lives — including happy memories of play and leisure, and everyday life activities of communication and relationship-building — tremendously difficult.

This Is What Inequality Looks Like

I have been saying for a few years now that the poverty story is the story people don't mind hearing, but the inequality lens is the one we actually need in order to better see what is going on.

What I suggest in my book, and today, is that we have tended to look at the challenges faced by kids from low-income households as if they are separate from the lives of kids from higher-income households. We have also tended to overlook the importance of social context in building family lives and in parental authority, and how, in raising youth, parents of different means are harnessing very different resources. Moreover, their practices and their strengths tend not to be recognised and rewarded in our society.

If we are serious about improving the lives of people such that everyone living in this society can meet their needs, we must look at the ways in which unequal conditions lead to unequal outcomes. The conditions must be where we place our attention to effect change, not the persons who are now in low-income circumstances.

I spend a lot of time in my book discussing the practices and norms among higher-income persons. And I spend a lot of time in the book discussing how access to various needs — housing and care support, for example — is deeply dependent on wage income, and how wage inequalities map onto people's access to public goods.

Hearing responses to my book over the past eight months, I know it continues to be hard to look inequality in the eye. It is more bearable to sidestep the question of inequality — which is essentially about the uneven and unfair distribution of resources — and go straight to the issue of what can be done to *help the poor*.

I have, in the past months, met many people and groups who are doing good work, who are very committed to helping the low-income, and who would like me to say to them that investing in early childhood education is the solution. We go around in circles in our conversations — them wanting to hear what I cannot say because I do not believe it to be true.

I, of course, do not have monopoly over truth. I can only say what I know from the data I have. From my research, I see that the barriers that kids from low-income families face have to do with the broader reward systems we all live in and the ways in which our system rewards some qualities and not others. These qualities can and are bought by money. The barriers kids face also have to do with their limited access to family lives, and that in turn has to do with the poor job conditions and low wages their parents face, and the consequences this has on families meeting all kinds of needs.

Focusing on inequality is uncomfortable because if the problem is the unequal distribution of things, then the solution has to be a more equal distribution of things. And this requires a great deal of undoing of our common sense about what it is our system now rewards and values, and a great deal of undoing what our society takes for granted about people's worth and deservedness.

Returning to the issue of children, these are the three things I think need to change.

First, our education system has to stop insisting on precocity and instead give children more time to learn and develop their varied strengths at a reasonable pace. This would benefit everyone — students, teachers and parents across class lines. Our education infrastructure is good — well-trained teachers, ample resource materials and buildings — it is possible for these to be widely enjoyed. Time must be the gift we grant kids to learn and teachers to teach.

Second, the well-being of kids and their parents are deeply intertwined. The wages of adults, their work conditions, and the access adults have to healthcare, to childcare support and to housing — these shape the everyday lives of families. Children make for good targets for interventions because of people's positive prejudices regarding their innocence, but they live in families, and the conditions faced by adults in the family matter greatly. We cannot separate thinking about the well-being of children from those of their caregivers. Adults' needs for better wages, better work conditions where they have better control over their schedules, and access to public goods that do not replicate market inequalities are crucial rather than secondary.

Third, when thinking about interventions and helping, we must think in terms of creating conditions that allow people mastery over their lives, that allow them to make the best decisions for their families. Interventions that are aimed at forcing people into a certain mould rather than giving people room to exercise agency will not meet needs.

A Moment of Possibility

I opened my talk with the claim that this is a moment of possibility. Now I'd like to close with returning to this.

As I mentioned, I have been very encouraged that people want to read and engage with my work. I am also noticing, however, some patterns in the many reactions to it that I think are constraints, roadblocks.

The first is a fear of disagreement and conflict, as well as limited space for genuine debate. No piece of work enters a vacuum. My book is born into a space that is not especially comfortable with disagreements nor especially comfortable with analysing evidence of the sort I have used in my book. I see people trying to have conversations, and I see challenges to these attempts. And I encounter the difficulty we have talking to one another, trying to comprehend each other using disparate mental frameworks and vocabularies. So, within this moment of possibility, the challenge around having conversations is two-fold. We have to keep trying to understand the issues better, but we also have to keep struggling to make space to talk about those issues in a civil way that allows for disagreement and understanding.

Over the past months, I also sense impatience. I recently realised that because this book is fairly easy to read, both readers and myself as a writer can forget that a lot of academic work went into it. I spent many years thinking about some key puzzles, trying to answer them in different ways, before I wrote this book. I am saying this because I think it's not obvious — that research takes time and is sometimes meandering, and that its purposes of resolving puzzles are not always solutions-oriented in the same ways that organisations are. I want to say this explicitly because I think we live in a world somewhat impatient for solutions. Our attentions are scattered, rarely sustained; we don't like to read long things and want things to be summarised. I am also a member of this impatient world, so I too am sometimes impatient for solutions.

Because of this book, I have been asked a lot about how we can come up with solutions, and I feel a certain urgency to respond to this call. But as a scholar, a major responsibility I have is to scrutinise, analyse and contemplate. And as a sociologist, in particular, I am always trying to turn things on their head, to get people to look at things using different lenses. With this work on poverty and inequality, I can see that as a society we have very deep prejudices and very deep instincts that are not easily overturned.

I can see people responding positively to my book in one moment, and, then in the next, going back to habits, to old frameworks and to common sense ways of thinking that are exactly the problems I've pointed to. So, my role, as I see it, is often to say, hey, let's slow down and ask what are we assuming about how individuals function here, what are we assuming about how power works and how changes come about. Can we think about the problem differently before we construct solutions? I do this because I think that if we frame questions in wrong ways, if we don't spend time thinking about how those questions should be answered, if we don't take the time to go deeply into explanations that are nuanced and sometimes contradictory, and if we don't do the hard work of examining and being willing to scrutinise our policies at the level of principles rather than at the level of delivery, our solutions will not be solved. And if we keep doing essentially the same things, we should not be surprised when things turn out essentially the same.

Question: Some people might feel that there's largely nothing wrong with our education system and it only needs tweaks at the policy level. What would patience with our education system look like?

Answer: When I said patience, I didn't mean that fundamental shifts do not need to happen. When I said patience, what I meant was precisely that there has to be a willingness to confront some of these fundamental principles. This takes a longer time and takes a more sustained engagement than just tweaking at the surface. I think that with education, there are two things. One is that the reward systems are fairly narrow and what they're rewarding are class advantages. We have a very good infrastructure in many ways, but because of the requirement for children to perform certain kinds of skills at a certain level (which are tested in standardised tests) and because those assessments are very high stakes, it's very difficult to get away from trying to cram as much as possible into kids.

One of the things that I've been thinking about a lot is that there is value in not cramming our children into little boxes; that is good for all kids and all parents and teachers, and not just narrowly for the low-income. We have this paradoxical situation where, on paper, we have a great school system and we do well on so many fronts. And yet when you talk to people, nobody seems to be happy and everybody seems to be hurting. Teachers seem to be hurting. Parents are hurting and, certainly, our kids are hurting. It doesn't seem to be rational that we continue hurting.

The other thing is that when I've had conversations with people about the school system, they tell me, "You know even if you change the system, parents are not going to behave differently." This is commonly brought up. I don't think that's true because if you just look at the changes to parental practices now, compared to ten years ago, and then compared to 20 or 30 years ago, parents respond to the context. Parents behave in the way that they behave because of the context. There's nothing fixed in parents' DNA that they won't behave in certain ways, and one of the reasons parents are very anxious across the class spectrum is because they know there are high stakes, they know the PSLE (Primary School Leaving Examination) is high stakes.

Parents want to behave in responsible ways and when they see that it's high stakes, meaning that it will lead to certain kinds of pathways, which in turn lead to different possibilities for meeting needs, then they're going to feel anxious and try to do the best they can and provide tuition and all those things. So, the education question is not separate from what inequality looks like at the end of the road. You can't detach the two. When you have a society where how you meet your needs (whether it's housing, healthcare, education, retirement security or any of those needs) is highly dependent on your wage work, and if wage work is highly dependent on the kind of credentials you have, you're going to try your best to make sure that your children do well in their exams.

This does not mean we just sit on our hands and not talk about solutions. I am very interested in having conversations with people in different fields and sectors, with experience and knowledge that I do not have, so that we can talk about how as a society we can do better than we have. I think part of what my academic approach implies is that in these conversations, I would also highlight the importance of continually moving back and forth — back and forth to talk about short-term goals and long-term hopes; back and forth between scales — what is possible for individuals and small groups of people to do, and what it is that has to be done on a societal scale.

Moving back and forth is important because sometimes there are actions that may move at cross purposes. What we do in the short term may harm what we want to achieve in the long term; what we do on a small scale may short-circuit what we want done on a large scale. These two are the principles for imagining solutions: first, paying attention to how problems are framed before jumping into solutions; second, moving back and forth between long and short terms and between small-scale and large-scale. I hope this will be useful to some of you in your work.

Finally, in this moment of possibility, I see a certain kind of pessimism and cynicism. I wrote about this in the preface of my book, and I have encountered it repeatedly over the past months.

People keep telling me: systems are too hard to change, let's focus on what community can do, what we as individuals can do, how charities and groups can step up, and let's not look to the government. On this, I find myself in the rather odd position, given my critiques of the state, of insisting that we do not become cynical about our public systems. Policies, regulations and laws — they shape our lives deeply and profoundly. Most of the conditions in which we as individuals make our decisions and live our lives are shaped through public policy. Without attention to these, no matter how much money we pour into other kinds of solutions, we will not be able to shift things in meaningful ways. When we look at the international research on inequality, we know that public policy is absolutely crucial for mitigating it.

I do think this is a moment of possibility. But in it, there are constraints and challenges. For it to be more than a moment of possibility, there is a great deal of work to do. I hope many of us will have the resolve, the commitment and the energy to work together in the years ahead.

CHAPTER FIVE

Parenting: Does One Size Fit All?

John M. Elliott

About the Speaker

The late Dr John M. Elliott was Associate Professor in Psychology at the National University of Singapore (NUS) and a Research Fellow for the local Bioethics Advisory Committee, before retiring in 2018. He passed away in 2019 after an unequal battle with prostate cancer.

Dr Elliott was born in the United Kingdom and came to Singapore at a young age, attending school in both countries. After graduating with Honours from the University of Cambridge in Experimental Psychology and obtaining his doctorate from the University of Sheffield, he joined the then Ministry of Social Affairs in Singapore as a Psychologist for three years. He then left to work in the UK and, after ten years abroad as an academic member of staff at the Department of Psychology at Sheffield, he returned to Singapore and joined NUS in 1986. This was the year when Psychology was first offered as an undergraduate subject at the university, as Dr Elliott recounts in his book *The Strange Start of Psychology at the National University of Singapore,*[1] which was posthumously launched at the end of 2021.

---

[1] John Michael Elliott, with assistance from Sim Tick Ngee, *The Strange Start of Psychology at the National University of Singapore* (Singapore: Department of Psychology, National University of Singapore, 2021).

As many would attest, he was loved by his students for his dedication in teaching Child Development and Evolutionary Psychology. His students were touched by his passion for children's welfare: Dr Elliott would devote an entire lesson to child maltreatment in his developmental lectures. They were often in awe of his vast knowledge, which went beyond his research interests and expertise. But they also in time came to appreciate him for his personal qualities.

Quah Saw Han, a clinical psychologist, remembers that he was always quietly supportive of her, taking time to touch base and explore opportunities for research collaboration. This was the reason why she was more than willing to help when he invited her to volunteer as a Research Advisor with the Singapore Children's Society. Cheung Hoi Shan, who worked with Dr Elliott as a Research Officer at the Society and was supervised by him as a doctoral candidate at NUS, too discovered that he was an exceptionally nurturing person, ever ready to welcome his university students and research staff members from the Society to his home for intellectual discussions on research. Both Saw Han and Hoi Shan came to regard him as a role model mentor.

Dr Elliott believed in doing research to address the needs of society and knowledge gaps in the local context. At his lecture on local parenting practices *Parenting: Does One Size Fit All?,* he cited a longitudinal study that was conducted by the research arm of the Society. The study found that placing toddlers in childcare or in the care of their grandparents was not more likely to be associated with poorer cognitive or social-emotional developmental outcomes at 3 years of age, than toddlers whose primary caregivers were their mothers. This speaks to the utility of local research findings and their role in guiding local childcare policy and caregiving decisions.

In his lecture, Dr Elliott emphasised that parenting behaviours may have meanings different from those in the literature, due to cultural differences in local parenting styles. He made a crucial point that struck a chord with Saw Han and Hoi Shan and, most likely, all the other psychologists in the audience. The wisdom from extant parenting literature is that children thrive when their parents encourage them to be independent and do so with emotional warmth. In contrast, children whose parents control their behaviours by setting non-negotiable rules and are emotionally unresponsive towards them may face difficulties in later life.

Asian parents set high expectations for their children and typically tend to express their concern in ways that make them "appear to lack warmth", as Dr Elliott aptly put it. His take-home message was that we cannot assume that a lack of emotional warmth is necessarily detrimental to children's development in the local context. We need data about local parenting styles and their impact on children's development before we can make such conclusions.

We are also not to throw the baby out with the bathwater. There are cultural-general patterns such as the role of mother-child attachment in children's early social-emotional development, but how toddlers take comfort from their secure base may differ from culture to culture, as Hoi Shan notes. Rather than assuming parents can only show concern by being warm to their children, we are instead invited in Dr Elliott's lecture to think about the importance of how children perceive their parents' concern.

Dr Elliott also raised the contentious and divisive topic that is corporal punishment in his lecture. He had observed that most of his students had experienced being caned but were reluctant to want to use it as parents. This echoes the findings of a recent study conducted by the Society in collaboration with Yale-NUS College.[2] In this study of local parents, most reported that they had been physically punished as a child. Most were against using physical punishment as the main method of disciplining their children, and a number expressed some regret after using it on their children. Yet many still used physical punishment.

---

[2] This is a forthcoming study tentatively titled *Parental Disciplinary Practices in Singapore*.

Local discipline practices are awkwardly juxtaposed with the United Nation's Committee on the Rights of the Child's recommendation to ban corporal punishment of children in all settings, in their concluding observations on Singapore's combined fourth and fifth periodic reports in 2019.[3] There is also a need to substantiate our public education initiatives with empirical evidence that takes into account the local cultural context. In words that Dr Elliott might have used, we are in need of more information about how local parents discipline their children, the factors that influence their decisions, and how these practices affect children's development. Over the years, under his stewardship, the thrust of the research done at Singapore Children's Society has sought to understand the context of raising children in Singapore.

With fingers in a staggering number of pies, it was impressive how Dr Elliott found time for his responsibilities as a long-time volunteer with the Singapore Children's Society as well as the Orchid Society of South East Asia (OSSEA), his job as an Associate Professor to both undergraduate and postgraduate students and his role as husband, father and grandfather to his family. Having first volunteered with the Society in 1974, he became a member of its Executive Committee in 1975 and subsequently chaired the Research Committee for almost 20 years, serving on a number of other committees within the Society at the same time. His involvement with the OSSEA spanned a similar number of years.

John Elliott at 8 years old.

Dr Elliott's legacy as a passionate, caring and inspiring person will be deeply felt in the years ahead. While he is best known for his contributions to society, he is most fondly remembered for his repartee and ability to defuse situations with his sense of humour.

---

[3] United Nations, Committee on the Rights of the Child, *Concluding Observations on the Combined Fourth and Fifth Periodic Reports of Singapore* (Geneva: United Nations, 28 June 2019).

The 13th Lecture, delivered 12 October 2019

It is a great honour for me to be actually asked to speak here. I have never, when moderating, thought of myself as somebody who ought to be on the other side of the table,[4] so it was a big surprise for me to be asked. But I will do my best to live up to expectations.

I want to make a preliminary comment about all this, which is that I am *not* going to address the question of how you deal with problems. I am assuming that we are talking about parents who have normal concerns and who want to do their best for their children. And I am assuming further that their children are by and large typical children. I am not addressing questions that might be raised about children with special needs or children with particular disabilities or problems that might require adjustments in parenting. So, really, what I have to say would be applicable very generally.

"Parenting is something you learn on the job. Books, in-laws, other relatives and friends are no substitute for the real thing." I am quoting Mr Koh Choon Hui, Chairman of Singapore Children's Society, who wrote the preface for the *Speaking of Children* book.[5] And I really believe that. I do think, and the tenor of my talk today is going to be very much that, parenting is something that you learn on the job and not something that you learn from books or from other sources. Now I am not going to keep you in suspense. What I am going to do is quite quickly go through five points that I want to make in this lecture and explain to you what they are, and I hope you will see where they are leading.

---

[4] Dr Elliott was the moderator for many of the Singapore Children's Society's annual lectures.
[5] Singapore Children's Society, *Speaking of Children: The Singapore Children's Society Collected Lectures* (Singapore: World Scientific, 2016).

In Singapore, we have parented our children in many different ways.

The first point is that both historically and right now until today in Singapore, we have parented our children in many different ways. We have different systems of child-rearing. We have different systems of discipline. The atmosphere, if you'd like, the style of different families can be very different. And this is, for perfectly good, understandable and practical reasons, culturally acceptable. But it is a fact. And I want to draw attention right away to the fact that parenting is very diverse. I further want to make a point that there isn't a very clear-cut distinction in my opinion between Western and Asian parenting generally and, in particular, Singaporean parenting.

But I *do* want to draw attention to what I think is a potential difference although there are lots of overlaps. I think it is necessary to say this because there is a strong tendency, an increasing tendency, for people to consult psychology textbooks and other things of that sort; writings that offer guidance and advice to parents on child-rearing which are of Western origins. And I have always told my students when I taught developmental psychology, parenting is one of those areas where you shouldn't assume that everything that you read about in textbooks that were written in America or the United Kingdom is necessarily true for Singapore. And this is partly because there are limitations in research on parenting and child-rearing. We don't have a lot of research into Asian parenting. We have very little research on parenting in Singapore. It's not that there is none, but we don't have that kind of comprehensive research base to draw upon. And some characteristics of Asian parenting may have been missed or misunderstood or underemphasised.

Now my fourth point is going to be that, given all the above, children do actually have definite needs; they are not indefinitely flexible. We are not free to do anything we like with children and assume it makes no difference to the outcome. It does make a difference to the outcome and what children's needs are should

©SPH Media Limited

Parents and other caregivers buying food for their 6-year-old children during recess on the first day of school, circa 1980s.
Source: The Straits Times © SPH Media Limited. Reprinted with permission.

inform parenting. But that doesn't imply, in my opinion, that there is only a single best way to rear children, that there is just one style of parenting or one way a family should approach the question of how you bring up your children. And therefore I come to the conclusion that Singaporean parents should perhaps have more confidence that they are the best judges of what is best in their own families. You can take information from experts or people in other fields or what is written here or there, anywhere and what friends and relatives tell you, but at the end of the day, you, the parents are probably the best judges.

Okay, now I want to elaborate on each of these points, but you can see where we are going with parents and our children in many different ways. When I first came to Singapore, it was quite common for children to be fostered out during weekdays, or for weeks, months or even years, with very limited contact with parents. The baby might have been put with another family and brought up as a toddler and never known much about his own family. That would be kind of extreme, but it happened quite a lot. And that was the alternative to bringing up children in the family home.

Today, of course, fostering refers much more to the care of children whose parents cannot properly care for them. But nowadays it is not considered a convenient way of sorting out how to manage your children. Historically, families were larger and it was sometimes difficult to keep the fourth or fifth child in the family, so the child was fostered out. But I think this was not a good system. This is one area where I would want to professionally say that fostering out is not a good idea and there are a certain number of adults to this day in Singapore who feel a little resentful, a little regretful that they were excluded from the family and didn't know it when they were growing up as children. But the context of fostering is very different now from what it was 50 years ago.

Question: What if parents have different opinions on raising their child?

Answer: I'm prepared to bet that Amy Chua's[6] husband was not a *Tiger* father before he met her. People tend to feel quite strongly about how they should bring up their children, and you may have a very happy relationship until the children arrive and you discover that there are different expectations between the both of you as to how to proceed and what should best be done.

I don't think there's any real solution here except to thrash this out and discuss this very thoroughly beforehand. You don't want to end up saying, "Oh, we have a kid. Now how are we going to bring the kid up?" Singaporeans are actually very good with planning, much better than in other places I

---

[6] Amy Chua, *Battle Hymn of the Tiger Mother* (New York: Penguin Press, 2011).

have known, so this is one of the things you should probably incorporate into your planning. So that you know you're on the same page.

I can admit that people often didn't do that in the past. I remember not discussing this very much with my own wife, which was not sensible. But luckily, we saw fairly eye-to-eye on most things, so it all worked out alright in the end. But it is true that if you have strong views, then you really need to thrash it out before you get to the stage of having children on hand.

The other thing I would say is that if you do have a disagreement, you need to settle it behind closed doors and not in front of the children. That's really important. You don't want to have a situation where you are arguing and the child sort of gets to understand that, "Oh well, Mummy will allow this, but Daddy will not allow, so I will always go to Mummy." And then the child plays off the parents one against the other. That's not good. Disagreements about how to manage children are not to be debated in front of the children.

Now another possibility you could say is, let's have babies or young children in the family, but let's have them under the care or responsibility of a live-in nanny or maid or babysitter. So, two exemplars of this immediately spring to mind. One of these was the use of *amahs* (阿嬤) to care for children. Now, these *amahs* were traditionally Cantonese and black-and-white-clad, the *ma jies* (妈姐), and they were in effect members of the family. They lived in the family and devoted very long periods of time as members of that family. They were servants, but they were in the family all the time. And their exclusive job was to look after the children. But they have passed with the passage of time and they were, to some extent, superseded or succeeded by the use of maids or nannies and both of these have some sort of pros and cons.

If we look first at the *ma jies*, the black and white *amahs*, they were not strict. All the people I have known who had anything to do with them, anything that came across from Kenneth Gaw's[7] excellent book, is that these were patient, loving caretakers. If there was going to be discipline involved, it was provided by the parents, not so much by these *amahs* who were very patient and very, very loving and very, very inclined to sway and cajole the children to do what they needed to do. And I took a quotation from Madam Tong Yuet Ching from the *Superior Servants* book, "You should not hit children. A girl I looked after was 4 when her father hit her for not eating her food. She said that it made her very angry then. She is 18 now but she has not forgotten."

Alright now of course with maids, the problem was a little bit different. I remember ten, 15, 20 years ago, there was quite a lot of concern about the use of maids, especially Filipino maids but not exclusively Filipino maids, as being a live-in childcare arrangement. This was because you actually had in the house somebody of a different culture trying to bring up the children according to what you wanted. But they too were a little bit, well, you couldn't be assured as in the case of the *amahs* that your maid was going to be a wholly dedicated person.

The other thing was that maids were usually not long term. It was a worry that children would be attached to the maid and would start to love their maids more than their natural parents. So, now I am happy to say that I don't think it is actually the nub of the problem. I think it is perfectly possible for children to have really good relationships with their parents and still have been brought up to a large measure at home by a maid. I should also

---

[7] Kenneth Gaw, *Superior Servants: The Legendary Cantonese Amahs of the Far East* (Singapore: Oxford University Press, 1988).

say that I am not talking exclusively about Filipino maids as there are maids from Indonesia, Malaysia, Thailand and Myanmar; this is a general observation. Because, as I am going to go on to show from some of the research done by the Singapore Children's Society, the relationship between the mother, in particular, and the child is what is really important for long-term outcomes in terms of the success of parenting. So, maids and *amahs* shared a tendency to be patient and loving rather than strict. Most parents wouldn't be too happy to delegate the idea of strict discipline to their maids and in fact they worry, still worry to this day, about the other way of children being spoiled and children developing a sense of entitlement as a result of being brought up by maids. And also there is a possibility of maids not turning out to be good caretakers. So, I think the verdict on maids as a method of childcare is a little bit open, but if managed right probably works okay.

Now the third possibility, I am still talking about the diverse ways in which we make arrangements for bringing up our children, is that you could rely on grandparents or other relatives to provide actual caretaking. With parents often absent at work, it makes a lot of sense as opposed to having the parents, which would normally mean the mother, provide the actual childcare. This is very common. It can also raise issues of disagreement over how to rear the children, especially if the parents see the grandparents as spoiling or over-indulging their grandchildren. That's the modern way of looking at it. If I go back 30 or 40 years, I think the problem was rather the other way around. Grandparents tended to have rather strict ideas about how children ought to be brought up and young mothers who have modern ideas from reading psychology textbooks on how to bring up their children would find themselves arguing with grandparents, with their in-laws, in particular, about being too strict. But it is the other way around now. The parents tend to feel that grandparents are spoiling their children and grandparents tend to say, well you know we are grandparents, we want to enjoy our grandchildren and not have to be discipline masters.

Question: What is the role of grandparents in bringing up our children?

Answer: You can't treat grandparents as necessarily available. We are having marriages later and later, which means that grandparents are going to be older and older; so some of them will have passed on. There will be children who are born who never know their grandparents. It's also the case that people are working longer and longer and leading active lives. I myself only retired last year at the age of 73, so I was a working grandfather for something like 13 years.

It becomes one of the things where, if you have grandparents available, they are a really useful resource, but you can't presume that grandparents are willing, necessarily, to set aside all their other activities, careers and interests just for the sake of grandchildren. Usually, grandparents are very keen to play a part in bringing up their grandchildren. But I have to say that it's nice to know that they're going to go back to their parents. Their parents are the people responsible, and they don't offload onto you the full responsibility. So, you can enjoy your grandchildren in a way that's a bit different from your own children.

I speak as a grandfather here. I really appreciate the fact that I have grandchildren. I really enjoy seeing them, but I wouldn't want to be the person responsible for making the decisions that their parents have to make on what to do about their education, about health and sickness, about any of the disastrous experiences they might have with friends in school and things like that. That's a matter for parents.

So I think the role of grandparents is to be in the background. They're there. They're a kind of emotional safety net. They're sometimes a financial safety net too. They're there. They want to be there. They want to be helpful, but they don't, by and large, or shouldn't anyway, want to run things. They want to enjoy their grandchildren and not feel that they have yet another job, which is to substitute for parents and bring up the children as if they were the alternative parents. Grandparents are not alternative parents, they are a backstop and a source of a lot of nice times in the family if relationships are good and harmonious.

Okay, now I come to something a little controversial. We don't just vary in how we bring up our children in terms of the arrangements we make, we have a lot of diversity in the dynamics of the parent-child relationship within the family. We also have a big range of disciplinary techniques ranging from corporal punishment (caning) and scolding to relying on persuasion, reasoning, and what I would call emotional control, appealing to the child's sense of right and wrong, a sense of guilt, a sense of what you ought to do, as being the basis on which you try to persuade the child to do the right thing. And very often these methods are mixed. It is rare to find anyone who relies on a single disciplinary method, but the emphasis varies tremendously from family to family.

Now physical discipline is quite a controversial topic. Caning has always been widely used in Singapore by Singaporean parents. I have asked successive cohorts of developmental psychology students in NUS, "Were you caned as a child?" And about 70% say yes. I then asked them, "Will you cane your children, if any?" and the answer was much less. They, having experienced it, weren't keen to perpetuate it on their children. The trouble is this figure of 70% did not change over the years. So, quite obviously when the students matured and were faced with the realities of what it actually means to bring up children, they found it helpful to have a cane in the house. And I have, many times, been challenged on this. People say it's a form of child abuse and, in many countries, it is considered a form of child abuse. In Scotland only two weeks ago, they banned smacking children; never mind using a cane, using a hand is also considered illegal now in Scotland.[8] But in fact, the empirical data are quite mixed. This is one of those areas where I wish we have more local research because a great deal seems to really depend on the spirit in which corporal punishment is used and the kind of extensive social acceptance it has. I give you one example from the research literature. I am trying wherever possible in this lecture to base what I say on research findings where there are any, but I am freely mixing in my personal opinions as well so you must feel free to challenge me on them when we come to the Q&A.

There is a well-known study which you will find if you google caning as a disciplinary technique or something like that in Wikipedia. Wikipedia has quite a big entry on caning kids. And there was a research done in the United States which studied families that were white Caucasian and black but were otherwise reasonably similar and followed the children from the age of 5 to 16 years.[9] And it looked to see, on one hand, children who were caned, paddled, smacked or given physical discipline, and on the other hand, those who were not, and how they turned out in terms of getting into trouble with the law, being juvenile delinquents, having problems in school and that sorts of things. And they found very interesting results. For the Caucasian families, physical punishment for the children was associated with more delinquency, more school problems and more likelihood of getting involved with the law. For the black families, it was the exact opposite pattern. It was the children who were given corporal punishment in one way or another,

[8] See, e.g., Libby Brooks, "Scotland becomes first country in UK to ban smacking of children", *The Guardian*, 3 October 2019. https://www.theguardian.com/uk-news/2019/oct/03/scotland-becomes-first-country-in-uk-to-ban-smacking-of-children.

[9] Jennifer E. Lansford, Kirby Deater-Deckard, Kenneth A. Dodge, John E. Bates and Gregory S. Pettit, "Ethnic Differences in the link between Physical Discipline and later Adolescent Externalizing Behaviors". *Journal of Child Psychology and Psychiatry*, 45 (May 2004): 801–812, DOI: 10.1111/j.1469-7610.2004.00273.x.

who were the ones least likely to be getting into trouble when they were adolescents.

When you think about it, there are two obvious reasons for this. The first is simply that in America if you are black, you are much more likely to be picked up by the police. You are much more likely to be targeted as being a potential delinquent. It is part of the price you pay at the moment still, I am afraid, for being black in the United States. So, it is important for parents to really impress on their children that you mustn't fall in badly with the law. There is a certain urgency about this for parents. But I think the other reason is that in the case of the Caucasian families it was seen by the children as rejection, it was seen by the children that "My parents don't love me. My parents are unfeeling; my parents are cold", whereas in the case of the black families, it was seen as evidence of concern. It was seen as evidence that the parents were worried about the children and that made all the difference to how it was perceived.

Now I think there is a very real argument against corporal punishment. I am not myself an advocate for one or the other. I don't actually think it is for people like me to tell parents what they ought to be doing. But I will draw attention to the fact that I don't think caning has any inherent merit. I have no time at all for people who say or imply that caning children once from time to time is somehow good for them, that it stiffens them up, improves their moral fibre and reminds them of their proper place in society. I have no time for that sort of argument at all. But I think the real argument against it is that once you make it normally acceptable, it becomes something that can easily go down a slippery slope. You can easily become an overuser if you are not a conscientious parent, you might find it too easy to fall back on caning. So, it's one thing to talk about caning as a judicious punishment, but it's another thing to find that it becomes something that is universally regarded as somehow desirable. It has no inherent merit and it opens the way for the slippery slope to child maltreatment. I personally don't think you need to cane children to bring them up perfectly well.

But as I said, I am not in the business of telling people what they ought to do, I am in the business of providing people with information that they can use in making decisions about their families.

So why are there so many different approaches to bringing up children? I think it is quite clear it is a practical matter and a necessity for working parents. It can be a matter of: is there caretaking help available? Can we afford it? The background of parents is important to know. Values are important in an Asian culture. Is obedience more desirable than creativity? If you go to any kind of preschool or nursery, they advertise creativity. You know it is wonderful. Everything is going to be about creativity, but that's very recent. Most parents would have said 20 years ago that obedience is far more important. Western influences and research have had an impact. So, we really have a tremendous variety for many different reasons.

But what I want to stress is there is not much evidence to suggest that the actual approach makes that much of a difference. And I have actually taken the trouble to quote a little bit of evidence at this point. Singapore Children's Society supports research and we did a longitudinal study over the years 2007 to 2014 when we followed up with children from infancy to about 3 or 4 years. And we thought we would find that there was a difference in outcome according to the caretaking arrangements. But in the end, only the closeness of the mother-child relationship seems to matter much. In *The Infancy Study*,[10] we measured temperament, a range of developmental outcomes and mother-child attachment. We measured it at 4 months, 18 months and 3 years old. This was done jointly with KK Women's and Children's Hospital.

We looked at who the main caregiver was and, of course, straight away out came the varying arrangements. We had some where

---

[10] *The Infancy Study: The Impact of Caregiving Arrangements on Early Childhood Development*, published in July 2019, was Singapore Children's Society's 12th research monograph.

parents were the main caregiver, some were the grandmothers, some were the nannies, some were the domestic helpers, some were other relatives, some was childcare and, in fact, that was the main caregiver for most of the time. And there were plenty of cases where it changed over time. And we thought at first that this might produce interesting results as to what was best. But our findings suggest there is no one *best* caregiving type. Parents can decide which best fits their children's needs while keeping in mind family circumstances and their available resources. Mothers, however, may wish to strengthen mother-child attachment by having a deeper understanding of and being more responsive to their children's needs because mother attachment was the one thing that seems to matter. And we did not expect this reassuring finding.

We also found that the mother-baby bond was related to social-emotional skills but not related to a lot of other things. So, in other words, of all the things that we looked at, problem-solving skills, fine and gross motor skills and personal social skills were not related to the mother-baby bond, but this was important for social-emotional skills. We found it hugely reassuring that it didn't actually matter too much what sort of caregiving arrangements you adopted, provided that the relationship between the mother and the child was a good one. And it didn't seem the case that mothers had any difficulty in maintaining a good relationship despite the fact that they were working. I would add that research everywhere does suggest that working mothers are not risk factors for problems with children. Happy mothers, who are happy because they are working and pursuing their careers, are better mothers than unhappy mothers who have given up their careers to spend all their time with their children, to put it in a nutshell.

So my first point was that historically and today we parented children in many ways and it appears from research that this does not reveal big differences in the outcome for at least some of these varying arrangements.

Question: Nowadays, more and more children are being taken care of in childcare centres, and some of them may even enter infant care centres very early in life as these are part of our society's support for working parents. What is your take on the role of childcare and infant care centres?

Answer: Higher quality care leads to better child outcomes. It is one thing to have childcare centres, it is quite another matter what actually happens inside the centres. Some childcare centres may have a lot of advertisements about creativity, early mastery of social skills and other skills that everybody deems as important. But when you investigate the actual teaching and care arrangements, they can turn out to still be very old-fashioned in a sense of, for example, very timetable schedules. The children's routines and activities are broken down half-hourly. It's very directed, very guided and very top-down.

It is quite important to try to pick childcare arrangements and childcare centres where there is much more emphasis on autonomy for the child. The child's tendencies, talents, interests and so forth need to be engaged. Having said that, if we go back to the 1960s and 1970s in the United Kingdom, for example, there was hardly any childcare. But it was immediately obvious when it was available that it was something good for the children. All the subsequent research on the establishment of childcare revealed that the children who went to childcare did better later in all sorts of dimensions. Their openness, their willingness to explore and try new ideas and so forth were much greater than children who had been kept at home because their parents were still preoccupied with the idea that mothers had to stay at home and look after the child.

> In a way, almost any childcare is actually good although it is likely that the quality of the interactions within the childcare centre makes a difference. And if you have the possibility of a choice, that's the sort of thing you should look for.

There is no clear-cut distinction between Western and Asian parenting generally, and Singaporean parenting in particular, but they are not quite the same either.

Now I want to move on to the question of whether there is a clear-cut distinction between Western and Asian parenting generally and Singaporean parenting in particular. Because that affects how we should address the question of, or what weight we should give to sources of information in textbooks or books on parenting — Dr Spock's books,[11] the textbooks of child psychology. Should we pay attention or should we assume they might not apply in Singapore?

I want to consider two possibilities when addressing this question of what's the difference, if any, between Western and Asian parenting. Now you would think that maybe *Tiger Parenting* is the one thing that must surely be a very Asian thing. Well, maybe. This term *Tiger Mom* (虎妈) is a term coined in 2011 by Amy Chua who wrote a book called *Battle Hymn of the Tiger Mother* in America and detailed how she brought up her children accordingly. Later she backpedalled a bit. She got such a lot of adverse reactions that she softened a little bit. But it is certainly quite clear what she had in mind, and it was, first of all, that parenting is strict and demanding. You expect the highest standards of your children.

---

[11] Dr Benjamin Spock was an American paediatrician whose books on child-rearing influenced generations of parents in the 20th century.

You demand high levels of academic achievement. You expect mastery of activities such as music or sports or ballet or all three.

But children are not allowed to say, no I don't want to do it. You are usually given a choice of violin or piano and if you say, no I want to play the triangle or the ocarina or some completely obscure instrument, this is not going to go down too well. You have a highly structured life programme. You tend to have a detailed timetable; the mother will have an hour-by-hour plot of exactly what the child is going to be doing on Wednesday at 7 o'clock and so on. And the children have very little autonomy. The children are not consulted about this very much; maybe a little bit on the choice of instruments or the choice of sports, but by and large the children don't have a great deal of say in all these. It does seem to be very effective in promoting academic success. It may lead, however, to low self-esteem and school adjustment difficulties in the long run because the children, as they get older, become increasingly aware that they are actually satisfying their parents' wishes but not necessarily their own wishes. So, it is a little bit ambivalent. However, the term *Tiger Mom* has entered the lexicon and you would think this has got to be an Asian thing, particularly in the Confucian tradition.

But *Tiger* aspirations are not new. The idea that you should prepare your children from the earliest possible age to be accomplished in as many ways as possible is a long-standing interest in Singapore. We have always been like this. Even so, the idea that you try to get your children into the best schools, into the best universities, get the best education you can and get the best sort of job that you can find is not unique to Singapore and is not unique to Asia.

And if that was not enough, we have also, locally, parenting that is apparently about as far from *Tiger* parenting as you could possibly get. Ho Kwon Ping, one of my predecessor speakers, during his lecture in 2011, gave a very delightful and frank account of how his dinner time was occupied by violent, vigorous debates because he and his wife, Claire Chiang, encouraged their children to ask questions. His was one of the best lectures I have heard actually. I really, really enjoyed it.

And here I have actually taken two quotes from his chapter, *Preparing Our Children for the World of Tomorrow*, in *Speaking of Children*. He says, "Asking *why* got me into enormous trouble with my teachers, who, I remember, always just told me to shut up and sit down." My teachers said the same thing by the way, so I really resonated with that. "But asking *why* was the reason the greatest scientists discovered unknown truths of the universe, or doctors conquered incurable diseases, or social activists liberated entire societies or races from colonial oppression or racial apartheid." Asking *why* is the last thing a *Tiger parent* would tolerate. The answer is *because I say so, okay?*

And this is a second quote, an even more interesting one, "We prepared our children to be independent. When my elder son reached 18 years of age, I gave him just a few hundred dollars and I asked him to take a plane to Hanoi by himself and spend a week there on his own without any friend or any plan. He did it and he was very happy and I think it opened him up to the fact that you can be, from very young, an independent person." Now, these would appear to be completely opposite approaches. We can have Western parents who are pretty *Tiger*-ish and we can have local parents who are pretty Western in the sense that they are encouraging their children to be independent.

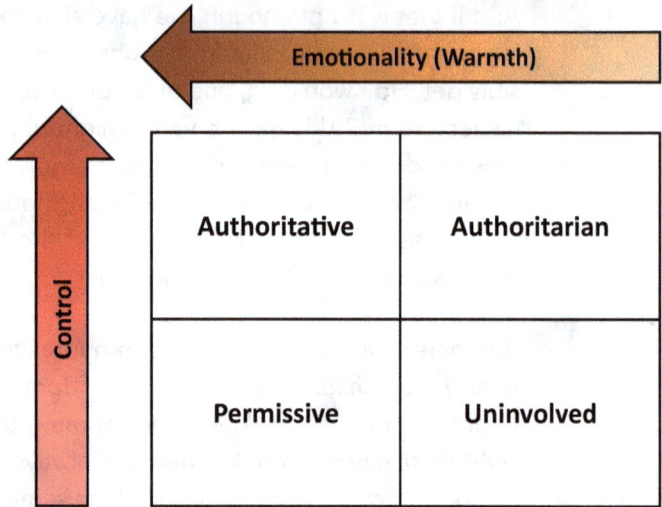

Dimensions of parenting adapted from Maccoby and Martin (1983)

So, what about parenting styles? Okay now I have to be a little bit technical, but I hope it will not be too bad. It's become traditional, meaning throughout the last 50 or 60 years, to break down parenting according to two, what I would call, dimensions.[12] If you look at the arrow along the top, what you are looking at is a dimension called *emotionality* which has, at one end, the idea that the parent is warm and responsive, and at the other end, the idea that the parent is rather unresponsive. I think rejecting is a bit strong, but that's the textbook term, so I can't change it. And then you have the *control* axis. So, parents on the bottom line are not very controlling, they are either warm, in which case they are considered permissive, or they are either rejecting and unresponsive, in which case they are considered uninvolved. On the top line, they are restrictive, they are demanding, and they have

---

[12] The diagram on the four parenting dimensions/styles is adapted from the work of two Stanford University researchers, who built on the earlier work of developmental psychologist Diane Baumrind. Eleanor Maccoby and John Martin, "Socialization in the Context of the Family: Parent-Child Interaction" in *Handbook of Child Psychology: Volume 4. Socialization, Personality, and Social Development*, eds. Paul Henry Mussen and Eileen Mavis Hetherington (New York: Wiley, 1983), pp. 1–101.

expectations that they insist upon. And they are either warm when they are doing it, in which case they are authoritative, or they are not, in which case they are authoritarian. And that actually, in a nutshell, is kind of a standard view.

Now, I think we can straightaway get rid of the bottom half. I don't think anybody is going to be arguing that permissive parenting or uninvolved parenting is a good thing. So, we will just consider this question of authoritative and authoritarian parenting. What distinguishes them? Now it seems to me obvious that somebody like Ho Kwon Ping falls into the authoritative category. Authoritative parents are warm, responsive but demanding. He did have expectations of his children; they had to go to Hanoi and survive on $500 for a week. And these parents tend to rely on inductive discipline, mainly on reasoning and appeal to conscience rather than fear. They tend not to run their families on the basis of *be afraid of me* but on other bases.

The *Tiger parent*, on the other hand, would be considered authoritarian in this scheme of things. They are also demanding, but they are neither warm nor responsive. They are very top-down, they are very *do as I say* in their approach. And they tend to use power assertive discipline, corporal punishment or nagging and scolding. Things that you know are insisting that the children do what they want but not granting much autonomy.

Now, is there anything that these two extremes have in common that tends to distinguish them as Asian parenting styles? We are at the nub now, at the meat so to speak. Because I think there is, actually. So, what might there be in common?

Some characteristics of Asian parenting may have been missed, misunderstood or underemphasised.

We are at topic three now. In my view, what these two examples have in common is a high, really high level of parental concern, and concern is not the same as warmth.

If you look at the parenting styles diagram again, it is showing you the contrast between warm, responsive parents and reject-ing, unresponsive parents. There is this idea that concern is somehow linked to warmth, but they can be delinked. You can be concerned without being warm. You can be warm without actually being very concerned. They are not synonymous; they are not the same thing. So, now we can see the possible differ-ence between Asian and Western parenting. In Western parent-ing, warmth has come to be seen as very important. This is in the last 70 years. If you go back to the middle of the last century, it was quite a different story. But now Western parenting consid-ers warmth important. Discipline inconsistent with warmth is seen as rejection and experienced by the children as rejection. Children go to school and say, my parents caned me, they are monsters.

In Asian parenting, concern is important. Discipline is accepted by and large as evidence of concern. And warmth is not a tradi-tional Asian value in a parent. If I think over the years, the number of times I have had parents say to me when I gave public talks like this on parenting, "But surely you can't expect, you know, you mustn't be too loving to your children, they will take advantage, they will climb all over you if you do that." So, warmth in the sense of being physically and emotionally warm within the family is not a traditional Asian value at all. But it is pretty much a traditional value now in Western parenting. I think that is actually quite an important difference. And one that makes me very cautious about attacking systems of parenting or styles of parenting that appear to lack warmth just on the grounds that they appear to lack warmth. There have to be other questions asked, such as is parenting doing what it should do and is it achieving the results it wants to achieve, rather than just worrying about how warm the relationship is.

The Needs of Children

Now, I do need to say something about children having definite needs and this should inform parenting, but this doesn't imply a single method. Now, what do I think the psychological needs of children are? I have listed what I think are the foremost important ones. Other experts may disagree slightly.

First and foremost, I think psychological security is really important. It is difficult for an adult to understand how chronic fear, anxiety and worry about the future can affect and undermine a child's sense of well-being. If you are worried that your parents might abandon you, and if they warn you that if you behave badly, they will give you away; we may joke about it as parents, but to children their parents are like gods, they have huge power. If you say something like that, the child takes it seriously. It really, really undermines the sense of security that they need in order to develop in other directions cognitively and socially. It's really paralysing to be suffering psychological insecurity especially if it's chronic when you are a child.

Number two. Have one or maybe a few adult figures that they are strongly attached to and whom they trust. It doesn't have to be the mother. It commonly *is* the mother, but it need not be. Over the many years, studies have shown that having one or a few figures that you really can rely on as a child, as an infant, is really important. This sense of trust adds to a sense of psychological security. The two things tend to go together.

Babies are smarter than you think. We now know because research in the last 20 years has shown that infants have got considerable cognitive abilities that they develop, that they don't tell us about because they can't talk very well. But they are there, and they develop by an opportunity to interact with the world in various ways. So, developing cognitively through play or other active experiences is important and that's what the root of this research on babies is, the root of all this emphasis in childcare provision on creativity and so forth. Babies need opportunities to develop cognitively and they need opportunities to interact socially with other children and adults. And if they have all these four things I've listed, then that sets a framework within which a lot of other things can vary on the details.

Question: What is your advice on the usage of technology, screens and all that, as part of parenting?

Answer: My own prejudice is to say that reading is important and hobbies are important and things that get you doing things with your hands are important. iPads and other gadgets get you doing things with your thumbs, but using the whole hand is important. You see, for people brought up as I was, long before the digital age, we had to entertain ourselves in various ways. We had toys, but we had toys that were construction toys that you built things with. I think there's a lesson there, which is that doing things is one of the ways children learn.

Hopefully, children can learn, before they are got at by the temptation of gadgets, that there are many interesting things to find out about the world. If you read and if you have little hobbies or activities that make you think, and preferably that use your hands as well, that's actually very good because you expand your mind, you learn to think, and then you'll be a little bit inoculated against the temptations of the screen.

It may not work. It may be that inevitably you will succumb because all your peers are succumbing, but I think it is better that parents generally take the view that we want to encourage our children to do things that are actually constructive forms of intellectual, physical and even emotional activities. This provides, to some extent, a foundation that you may lose sight of from time to time but, in the end, you'll come back and appreciate.

Concluding Points

Singaporean parents may need a bit more confidence that they are the best judges of what is best in their own families. And I say this because families differ. The personalities and temperaments of parents and children vary. Children may have special needs. Parents may have to juggle many responsibilities. Parents have many other things on their minds besides their children. It's not easy to be a parent.

Western parenting is predicated on the assumption that warmth is the essential ingredient in parenting. But in my opinion, concern is more important than warmth. I won't be popular in some places for saying that, but I think it is true. There is not much research on Asian parenting and even less on Singaporean parents. We need more research. And children and infants do have their definite needs and they should inform parenting. Parents should know about the existence of these needs and their importance, but it does not mean there is a single best or only way to rear children.

CHAPTER SIX

A Shared Journey
Safeguarding Our Children

Priscilla Lui Tsang Sun-Kai

About the Speaker

The youngest daughter in a family that treasures children, Mrs Priscilla Lui Tsang Sun-Kai was raised by her parents and her grandmother. She has always been grateful that her parents never left her unattended as a child nor were they ever harsh or abusive to her and her six siblings. Her father taught at Hong Kong University, while her mother, who spoke Russian, worked at a Christian organisation assisting migrant Russians from China. Her experience of growing up in a caring and cohesive family within a safe and non-violent environment, as well as her beliefs as a Christian, had a significant impact on her views about the protection of children.

Mrs Lui is the former Chairperson of the Hong Kong Committee on Children's Rights. Trained in the disciplines of Sociology, Criminology and Social Work, she has amassed more than 30 years of experience in child protection and the advocacy of children's rights in Hong Kong. She joined Against Child Abuse (ACA) — a charity in Hong Kong which provides quality child protection services and strives to eliminate all forms of child abuse — as its first full-time paid Administrator in

1979 and subsequently took on the role of Executive Director in 1983 before stepping down in 2011.

She has received numerous awards for her work, among them the Junior Chamber International Hong Kong's Ten Outstanding Young Persons Award in 1990, the Bronze Bauhinia Star Award in 2000, the Distinguished Service Award from the International Society for the Prevention of Child Abuse and Neglect (ISPCAN) in 2006, the Hong Kong Humanity Award from the Red Cross in 2009 and the Hong Kong Paediatric Society Child Health Medal in 2018. The author of two books, *Listen to the Voice of the Wounded Children*《听受伤的孩子在说话》(2011) and *Child at Heart*《说童心》(2017), she has also published in peer-reviewed journals on the topic of family violence and child abuse, and been a keynote speaker at international conferences including the 17th ISPCAN International Congress in Hong Kong.

When ACA was under her stewardship, she was responsible for introducing Hong Kong's Anti-Spanking Day and for driving the campaign to ban corporal punishment in Hong Kong. The impact of her work has not been unfelt in Singapore. *KidzLive: I Can Protect Myself* — a Singapore Children's Society programme which empowers children with body safety skills — was inspired by ACA's child sexual abuse prevention programme after ACA hosted a study trip in 1999 for staff and committee members of the Children's Society.

Due to pandemic restrictions, Mrs Lui gave her lecture, *A Shared Journey Safeguarding Our Children*, on an online platform. This marked our first virtually-held lecture and enabled us to reach out to an even wider audience, regionally as well as internationally. In her lecture, she argued for the need to install a Child Commissioner to champion children's best interests, to instate a Child Policy that realises the United Nations Convention on the Rights of the Child (UNCRC), and to recast Child Law in view of the UNCRC. These best practices reflect a gradual shift that Mrs Lui has perceived. There has been a movement from solely helping families secure children's basic physical and material needs, to society implementing policies and statutes that address children's rights, including their right to develop optimally and their right to autonomy of thoughts and feelings.

Perceptions have changed: the modern world views a child's well-being as not just a family affair, but "a shared journey and responsibility" of the community, Mrs Lui reflects. To this end, she highlights the need for agencies to replace piecemeal efforts with collaborative action. She perceives the need for a transparent, sustainable and multidisciplinary platform to work towards a common goal and to establish consistent practices. This, along with statutory support, resources and dedicated

Priscilla Lui as a 3-year-old.

personnel, would ensure that children's views and perspectives are holistically represented, she contends.

The way forward, Mrs Lui suggests, involves parents playing the role of advocates. Encouraging abuse survivors — parents who themselves have experienced violence and/or harsh treatment — to share their experiences has helped them understand their own difficulties and challenges. Rather than have ACA be the advocacy driver, testimonies by adult survivors and past abusers have been singularly effective in helping society understand the traumatic impact of abuse on children. Looking ahead, getting children and young people to be their own advocates is the next step, Mrs Lui feels.

The 14th Lecture, delivered 28 August 2021

Singapore Children's Society has been a good friend for the past 30 years. Thank you for treating me as family for, among the 14 speakers of your past annual lectures, I seem to be the only speaker from outside Singapore. What a big honour. Deeply appreciated!

The title, jointly chosen, *A Shared Journey Safeguarding Our Children*, is of paramount importance at this critical moment for us all.

The world is shivering. It is breaking down. The pandemic has been truly a catastrophic global crisis, the first of its kind in our lifetime that is shaking the world up, breaking the world down and gravely affecting everyone, our children in particular. Children suffer, many silently, and their survival, development, human relationship, mental health, care and education have all been seriously threatened.

In this lecture, I will share with you five major areas, based on international and Hong Kong experience.

Threats and Pressing Needs of Children's Rights and Well-being

To start with, prior to and after the onset of the pandemic's challenges, and especially looking at psychological well-being and online threats, Covid-19 is truly the first global crisis to this devastating degree that we have witnessed in our lifetime.

Save the Children's study[1] of 46 countries found that Covid-19 had adversely threatened the holistic well-being of children and

---

[1] Lavinia Loperfido and Melissa Burgess, *The Hidden Impact of COVID-19 on Child Poverty* (London: Save the Children International, 2020). https://resourcecentre. savethechildren.net/pdf/the_hidden_impact_of_covid-19_on_child_poverty.pdf/; Daniela Ritz, Georgina O'Hare and Melissa Burgess, *The Hidden Impact of COVID-19 on Child Protection and Wellbeing* (London: Save the Children International, 2020). https:// resourcecentre.savethechildren.net/pdf/the_hidden_impact_of_covid-19_on_child_protection_ and_wellbeing.pdf; Nicole Dulieu and Melissa Burgess, *The Hidden Impact of COVID-19 on Child Rights* (London: Save the Children International, 2020). https://resourcecentre. savethechildren.net/pdf/the_hidden_impact_of_covid-19_on_child_rights.pdf/.

their families in different ways. Their study interviewed 13,477 children aged 11 to 17, and 31,683 parents and caregivers. More than three in four households (77%) indicated that their families encountered income loss since the start of the pandemic and 38% had family members who were unemployed. Seventeen percent of the households which encountered income loss had a child who reported experiencing violence at home. Fifty-four percent of the children shouldered more household chores and 48% undertook more care duties towards their siblings and others. Regarding mental health, 83% of children reported an increase in negative feelings, about 74% were more worried, 62% were more unhappy and 47% felt less hopeful. As for educational opportunities, about 50% of the children lost access to learning material. Fifty-four percent were deprived of social interaction with their friends and peers, while 35% indicated they had no space to play.

An outdoor playground cordoned off at the height of Covid-19 restrictions in Singapore, May 2020.
Source: The Straits Times © SPH Media Limited. Reprinted with permission.

The Foundation of Women's Rights Promotion and Development shared their concerns on gender inequality. Women as main caregivers experienced domestic and sexual violence, and reports from the government and non-governmental organisations (NGOs) found a drastic increase in cases received and suspected that many more are hidden.

A study by the Hong Kong Council of Social Service on 5,900 service users found that 90% of the respondents were unemployed or under-employed and had suffered income reduction; half of whom had their income reduced by 50%. Seventy percent of respondents who suffered chronic illnesses worried about infection and thus either reduced their frequency of or entirely stopped their medical consultation or treatment. Sixty-five percent of respondents encountered hardships in their children's schooling and felt anxious.

Another study by the Hong Kong Society for the Protection of Children[2] interviewed 449 parents with children under 3. Ninety-three percent worried that their children would be adversely affected because they were staying home for a long time. Eighty-three percent felt like they were struggling and being tied up. Sixty-three percent observed poor emotional changes in their children. Forty-one percent of parents said their children enjoyed less than 30 minutes of outdoor activities every day. Thirty-eight percent of parents said their 2- to 3-year-olds' major activities were on electronic devices. The guidelines by the World Health Organisation (WHO) indicate that it is not suitable for under 2-year-olds to have contact with electronic devices such as iPads and mobile phones, while device use for 2- to 4-year-olds should not exceed one hour per day.

---

[2] [疫情下無得出街玩 2-3 歲幼兒近 4 成最常看電子屏] (Hong Kong: Hong Kong Society for the Protection of Children, 2 April 2020).

Globally, advocates have pointed out specifically that the pandemic has increased the social, economic and gender imbalance. Vaccine injustice, the widening gap of poverty and the increase in military expenses are threats to world peace.

Many studies have alerted us to see a code red for humanity, that our society is on fire. Human activity is upending the climate in unprecedented and sometimes irreversible ways. Crimes against Mother Nature are termed ecocide, which is as shameful as genocide. A call, loud and clear, to all of us is that only with immediate combined forces can such catastrophes be averted.

The United Nations Children's Fund in their new report alerted that climate crisis is a child rights crisis. The government must invest to reduce greenhouse gas emissions and to provide children with adequate education and support in environmental protection.

On top of the challenge of climate change, many problems threatening the optimal growth and development of children have lingered on for a long time. Covid-19 has exacerbated the risks and harm done to children and society. The impact will reverberate for a long period, threatening the optimal growth and development of children, the future of our society.

Children want us to see what they see, to listen to what they have to say, to feel the way they feel, to speak up for them, to stop the violence, to make them visible and be their advocates. For all these years, some important rights of children have been left unaddressed, threatening their survival, growth, development and participation.

Let me start with psychological well-being. WHO data in 2017[3] estimated that 300 million people have depression. They predicted that from 2020 onwards, depression would be second to coronary disease as the major burden in terms of sickness.

As early as 2002, the Hong Kong Family Health Service's Department of Health[4] had already indicated that 10% of 4-year-olds displayed behaviour with potentially significant psychopathology, while 10% to 15% of preschool-aged children had mild to moderate behavioural problems. A 2015 Hong Kong study on depression[5] found that 51% of secondary school students had depressive symptoms.

Intensive early intervention must receive policy and funding support. A 12-year longitudinal Hong Kong study of 1,000 patients with symptoms such as hallucinations or delusions found that intensive early intervention programmes for psychosis that were conducted in the first two years after diagnosis could cut down suicide rates by 50%. But Hong Kong has a shortfall of 400 psychiatrists, according to WHO standards. In Hong Kong, one case manager shoulders about 80 patients, whereas in progressive countries, one case manager would have about ten to 20 patients. Sadly, some children have to queue up over a year for diagnosis and treatment.

The Hong Kong Legislative Council's Welfare Panel on Health Service reviewed mental health concerns, and a Standing Advisory Committee on Mental Health was appointed in 2017. It

---

[3] *Depression and Other Common Mental Disorders: Global Health Estimates* (Geneva: World Health Organisation, 2017). https://apps.who.int/iris/bitstream/handle/10665/254610/WHO-MSD-MER-2017.2-eng.pdf.

[4] Shirley SL Leung, Cynthia M Leung and Ruth SM Chan, *A Needs Assessment Report of Children 0-5 Years* (Hong Kong: Department of Health, Family Health Services, 2005). https://www.fhs.gov.hk/english/archive/files/reports/report.pdf.

[5] "New study finds that more than half of Hong Kong secondary students are depressed". *South China Morning Post*, 1 September 2015. https://www.scmp.com/yp/discover/news/hong-kong/article/3071814/new-study-finds-more-half-hong-kong-secondary-students.

came up with 40 recommendations in 20 areas. The Committee in 2019 started to study the mental health condition of children and adolescents. The government also increased child capacity-building programmes by growing the number of parent resource centres from six in 2017 to 19 in 2020. And since 2019, NGOs in Hong Kong have initiated October as Mental Health Month. Dementia-friendly programmes have been introduced. And a group of young people have introduced the *Just Feel* programme to encourage parents and children to speak up.

The United Kingdom has conducted innovative mental health programmes such as *Time to Change*. Australia, with three million people living under anxiety or depression, has launched their *Beyond Blue* programme, and New Zealand in their *Like Minds, Like Mine* programme has been working against mental health stigma.

Another significant area left outstanding is the problem of online safety and negative exposure to the virtual world, a huge threat which has been exacerbated by the pandemic.

A study in the early 2000s by an NGO, Against Child Abuse[6] (ACA), interviewed 1,716 Form 1 to 3 students and found that 64% had come across obscene and indecent materials. Twenty-seven percent of them had received child pornography, 55% had contacted strangers known online and 39.4% had actually met these strangers.

Let me share some serious cases reported in the Hong Kong news. A 15-year-old girl who got a modelling job online was brutally killed and raped. A boy who was constantly bullied online was traumatised and, instead of seeking help and informing the authorities, took his own life. A helper was jailed for three months for publishing videos of naked children under her care, in the

---

[6] [网络活动对初中学生的影响] 调查报告 (Hong Kong: Against Child Abuse, 2004). https://www.aca.org.hk/top-cpci/survey/internet_survey.pdf.

shower. A 10-year-old girl who spent hours each day online during the Covid-19 lockdown met a stranger online who claimed to be as young as she was. He convinced her to take and send him nude photos and to provide the contacts of her friends for such materials to be circulated. One of her classmates' parents found out about it and reported the case to the police.

Children, particularly during Covid-19, encounter tremendous stresses and challenges online. Their physical, psychological, social and spiritual well-being have been falling apart. Parents and caregivers, teachers and professionals have been neither fully prepared nor supported.

Reports indicate that one in three internet users is a child.[7] Unwanted sexual comments, harassment, sextortion and bullying online are frequently found. Digital safety education is a must and coordination among law enforcement, schools and internet providers is essential. To rebuild the virtual world, the government, the information and communications technology industries, educators and parents must share the journey by addressing these challenges.

Advocates have recommended the setting up of a dedicated hotline to the Hong Kong government — a dedicated hotline with trained personnel to receive reports and render assistance to children, families and caregivers. Schools need to upgrade their child safeguarding policy to reflect current needs and practices. Parents should be guided to upgrade to the latest software and antivirus programmes, engage in dialogue with their children, set rules for usage, be alert to signs of distress, familiarise with local services and be ready to seek help.

The most recent initiative for children by the tech giant Apple has been a plan to scan iPhones in the United States for child abuse

---

[7] Sonia Livingstone, Jasmina Byrne and John Carr, "One in Three: Internet Governance and Child Rights", *Innocenti Discussion Papers no. 2016-01* (New York: United Nations Children's Fund, 2016).

images on the internet which, if found, might be reported to law enforcement bodies for follow-up action.[8] This may be a controversial initiative, as some people have been concerned about freedom of speech, yet, in the sense of child protection, it appears to be a positive measure worth active consideration.

For a shared journey to be possible, a constructive change in mindset, balancing children's and adults' best interests, must be put in place. Visionary leadership to champion for children and make children visible in policy, budget administration and practical sense is essential.

A Platform for Children: A Children's Commission to Champion for the Best Interest of Children and Make Them Visible in All Aspects

With reference to the United Nation's standards and stipulations, an effective champion for children, a Child Ombudsman or Child Commissioner, should head a statutory commission which is supported by its own team of staff, with funding for research and programmes. It must also be independent, transparent and sustainable. Community, especially children's, participation must be a pre-requisite for effective actualisation of its obligations under the UNCRC.[9]

A mechanism of this kind is not new. Norway, the true pioneer, started the first Ombudsman office in 1981. The lady who headed the mission considered children as true experts, regularly met with them and listened to their sharing and recommendations. The office took up cases reported and initiated studies and investigations of children suspected of being at risk or harmed.

---

[8] Following widespread concerns about privacy invasion, Apple decided in September 2021 to postpone its plans to roll out this detection technology.
[9] *Convention on the Rights of the Child* (Geneva: United Nations, 2 September 1990).

The functions of the Ombudsman or the Commissioner include the following:

- Formulating or amending policy and legislation
- Looking into unjust situations on behalf of children and families
- Having free access to child institutions and information, in order to trace trends, characteristics and contributing factors impacting children's best interests
- Ensuring education and promotion in child rights and child protection
- Ensuring a quality child protection system for children
- Monitoring and measuring progress

The UNCRC was passed in 1989, made effective in 1990 and ratified by almost all countries except the US. The British government had extended the CRC to Hong Kong in 1994, and the government of China extended the CRC to Hong Kong in 1997. On 1 June 2018, Hong Kong set up a Commission on Children, an advisory body with all government bureaus represented, and appointed 21 non-official members. Advocates continue to appeal for a statutory body that is independent and sustainable.

Currently, the world has at least 79 countries with a Children's Commission, 30 of them being independent children's commissions and 49 under human rights institutions.

Policy, Laws and a Proactive Child Safeguarding System

A Child Policy and an Action Plan

To ensure a genuinely shared journey for all, a child policy must be written down and made widely known as the direction of

society. It must be supported by a holistic and proactive action plan and an effective system to implement and monitor. To trace trends, characteristics and root causes, evidence-based studies must be conducted. Channels for public and children's voices must be properly put in place. Effective advocates must be identified for consensus-building and to ensure recognition, solidarity and empowerment.

The Committee on the Rights of the Child issued 11 child rights-based measures[10] in 2020 to encourage states to tackle the public health threat posed by the Covid-19 pandemic:

1. Consider the health, social, educational, economic and recreational impacts of the pandemic on the rights of the child.

2. Explore alternative and creative solutions for children to enjoy their rights to rest, leisure, recreation and cultural and artistic activities.

---

[10] *The Committee on the Rights of the Child warns of the grave physical, emotional and psychological effect of the Covid-19 pandemic on children and calls on States to protect the rights of children.* (Geneva: United Nations, 8 April 2020). https://tbinternet.ohchr. org/Treaties/CRC/Shared%20Documents/1_Global/INT_CRC_STA_9095_E.docx.

3. Ensure that online learning does not exacerbate existing inequalities or replace student-teacher interaction.

4. Activate immediate measures to ensure that children are fed nutritious food.

5. Maintain the provision of basic services for children including healthcare, water, sanitation and birth registration.

6. Define core child protection services as essential and ensure that they remain functioning and available, including home visits when necessary, and provide professional mental health services for children living in lockdown.

7. Protect children whose vulnerability is further increased by the exceptional circumstances caused by the pandemic.

8. Release children in all forms of detention, whenever possible, and provide children who cannot be released with the means to maintain regular contact with their families.

9. Prevent the arrest or detention of children for violating State guidance and directives relating to Covid-19, and ensure that any child who was arrested or detained is immediately returned to his or her family.

10. Disseminate accurate information about Covid-19 and how to prevent infection in languages and formats that are child-friendly and accessible to all children.

11. Provide opportunities for children's views to be heard and taken into account in decision-making processes on the pandemic.

To facilitate actualising policy and framework, the KidsRights Index's 2021 report[11] also listed five domains and seven selected indicators.

---

[11] Karin Arts, Dinand Webbink and Chandrima Chattopadhyay, *The KidsRights Index 2021 Report*. (Amsterdam: KidsRights, 2021). https://files.kidsrights.org/wp-content/uploads/2021/06/03095317/KidsRights-Index-2021-Report.pdf.

The five domains are as follows:

1. Right to Life

2. Right to Health

3. Right to Education

4. Right to Protection

5. Enabling Environment for Child Rights

The seven selected indicators are as follows:

1. Non-discrimination

2. Best interests of the child

3. Respect for the views of the child and child participation

4. Enabling national legislation

5. Mobilisation of the best available budget

6. Collection and analysis of disaggregated data

7. State and civil society cooperation for children's rights

In 2015, the Hong Kong Paediatric Society and Hong Kong Paediatric Foundation together with child healthcare professionals compiled a proposal on Child Health Policy for submission to the government. The proposal came into being with four drafting groups, six public forums and numerous professional consultations. Now, the report is in the hands of our Commission on Children for review.

A Sound Child Protection System

Policy will remain as a policy unless a sound implementation system is put in place.

In the best interests of children, a specialised child protection system has been put in place in Hong Kong, and it started in

1983 with a hotline piloted by the ACA. The Hong Kong government provides specialised services under the Social Welfare Department's Family and Child Protective Services Unit. Hospitals have child abuse medical coordinators. The police have a Family Conflict and Sexual Violence Policy Unit. In our courts and Department of Justice, we have prosecutors.

To monitor policies and practices, a working group, later upgraded to a Committee on Child Abuse and chaired by the Director of Social Welfare, shoulders an advisory role of monitoring policies and practices.

In December 2011, Hong Kong introduced the Sexual Conviction Record Check system under the Hong Kong Police Force to provide employers with a channel to ascertain applicants for work relating to children or mentally incapacitated persons, to ensure they have no sexual conviction records. However, the system is non-compulsory and not all-inclusive.

We need data to understand trends and characteristics, for service planning and budgetary allocation. Hong Kong is in the process of conducting a feasibility study on a central data bank to consolidate the different records and registries so that they are more consistent, inclusive and efficient in retrieving data and statistics for planning support for children and families, as well as for resource allocation.

What is fundamental in getting the field together is an effective and non-bureaucratic system operated by passionate, devoted, well-trained multidisciplinary personnel with adequate manpower, resourced and supported by quality management and supervisory personnel — through the case management process with stakeholders', particularly children's, participation.

Prevention is as important as cure. For a system to be preventive, a three-level intervention system must be properly put in place, with the top of the triangle being tertiary, to identify and work with those harmed or adversely affected. The secondary level is to identify early and work with those at risk. And the primary level for total reform is to impact values, mindsets and culture for children.

Question: We are individuals, but we're also neighbours, relatives, or somebody in the vicinity and we might see or hear something that we feel could potentially be of concern. How can we, as individuals, help to detect possible cases of child abuse in the community?

Answer: We have to always bear in mind the fine line of not intruding into family affairs. Though we are advocates for child rights and child protection, we shouldn't step too easily into the jurisdictions of other people, into family affairs. But at the same time, it shouldn't stop us from really paying attention to children's and families' needs. With some families, due to the lack of support, things do happen; some of them are drastic to the extent of harming a child or taking a child's life. So, we have to learn how to find a particular balance. This is being done over the years, through community education and self-awareness.

Let me cite an example of a supermarket worker who, though was very busily engaged in her work, found a child lingering in the neighbourhood. The child was emaciated and shivering. And so, the supermarket worker put everything down and tried to understand better from the child what was happening, who the child's guardians were, whether the child was alone, and so on. She eventually found that the child was in a desperate and risky situation, so she took the liberty and courageously brought this particular child to the attention of the police force.

After the child was taken to the hospital, the hospital personnel found that the girl was seriously anaemic to the verge of dying. I'm raising an extreme case and we may not see this very often, but it is possible for our general public to identify children who have been harmed if we are being supported in terms of values, knowledge and skills. The most important thing is that we are passionate about people around us, especially our little ones; that makes the shared journey even more important. It's not only for the professionals in the hospitals, in the social service agencies, or in the schools, but also for all of us to see that we have a role to play in the community.

Child Law as Society's Baseline

For any system to be effective, statutory support as the baseline is essential. The law has educational and directional value, and it helps to protect the rights and well-being of citizens — adults and children alike. It sanctions those who violate the law and deters future violations. Advocates in Hong Kong have persistently appealed to the government to conduct a comprehensive review of child-related ordinances and to formulate a children's act which incorporates the stipulations of the UNCRC.

Hong Kong in 2003 amended the Child Pornography Ordinance to criminalise those who possess, in addition to produce and disseminate, child pornography — actual and virtual images alike. Sentencing guidelines have also been drawn up to tackle various degrees of sanctions.

More proactive reforms in law have taken place in different parts of the world. Some examples include UK's Children's Act, which was introduced in 2004, and UK's Children's Commission, which was set up as a result of a huge outcry for little Victoria Climbie, an 8-year-old who died a tragic death.[12] UK has also made it a

---

[12] Victoria Climbie suffered horrific abuse from her great-aunt and her great-aunt's boyfriend. Her death brought to light the negligence of the relevant authorities and social services, and led to significant changes to the child protection system in the UK.

crime if one caused the death of a child, or should have known the child was at significant risk of serious harm and failed to take reasonable steps to prevent it. Similar laws have been enacted in South Australia and New Zealand.

In UK and Australia, witnessing domestic violence is defined as abuse and children are protected by law. More recently, Scotland has voted stipulations from the UNCRC into their child law.

As to the banning of corporal punishment, there are at least 62 states that have banned corporal punishment in all settings, including at home. Twenty-seven other states have made commitments to do the same.

Sweden, a true pioneer, banned corporal punishment in 1979. New Zealand banned it in 2007; their rate of approval of corporal punishment has dropped from more than 90% in 1981 to 40% in 2013.[13] Scotland banned corporal punishment in 2019, although its impact has yet to be measured.

You may wish to refer to the Global Report 2019 by the Global Initiative to End All Corporal Punishment of Children,[14] to better understand the rationale and progress. The Global Partnership to End Violence against Children's implementation guidance, published as part of the Together to #ENDviolence, Solutions Summit Series,[15] may also be inspiring as the foundation for a non-violent childhood, putting the prohibition of corporal punishment of children into practice.

---

[13] Beth Wood, *Physical Punishment of Children in New Zealand — Six Years After Law Reform* (New Zealand: EPOCH New Zealand, 2013). https://epochnz.org.nz/images/2013_Physical_punishment_of_children_in_New_Zealand_2.pdf.

[14] *Global Report 2019: Progress Towards Ending Corporal Punishment of Children* (London: Global Initiative to End All Corporal Punishment of Children, 2020). http://endcorporalpunishment.org/wp-content/uploads/global/Global-report-2019.pdf.

[15] *Laying the Foundation for Non-Violent Childhoods: Putting Prohibition of Corporal Punishment of Children into Practice: Implementation Guidance* (New York: Global Partnership to End Violence against Children, 2021). https://endcorporalpunishment.org/resources/implementation-guidance-2021/.

The banning of corporal punishment must start now. To urge the Hong Kong government to close the gap, by a total ban of corporal punishment, advocates have made special efforts every year on 30 April, International Anti-Spanking Day. One campaign effort, made in 2008, involved presenting a declaration with the signatures of 10,000 individuals and agencies to the government. The declaration specifies that violence comes in different forms. The corporal punishment of children is a form of violence and a violation of children's rights. It is necessary to set the same standards that apply to adults. While there is nothing wrong with child discipline, there are better non-violent means to guide and to teach.

Question: There seems to be a fine line between discipline and abuse. What practical advice would you give to parents about the discipline of young children?

Answer: I would like to emphasise that physical, corporal punishment is not the only way to discipline. The call for a total ban of corporal punishment has become a universal concern. You might start with a hit and you wouldn't call it abuse, but the hit in itself may eventually lead to more hits and more serious injuries. The reason that you hit your child is for the child to remember, for the child to know that you have a message and, if that message is not strong enough, you might use a stronger message.

When you use corporal punishment, you may cause pain and shame, and it may adversely affect your relationship with your child as well. A parent is a significant person in a child's life. But with corporal punishment the child learns, even at a fairly young age, that this significant person is hitting, and the child might easily take that as acceptable behaviour. And if the child displays such behaviour outside of the home and hits others, then the parent must reflect and ask themselves where the child might have learnt such behaviours from.

We all want our children to change certain behaviours that are not acceptable. But the question is what kind of approach should we use? What kind of attitude should we take? The time we use for our rethinking and reflection is important. However, because as parents we are often busy with other matters, it becomes too easy and spontaneous for us to fall back on corporal punishment. If we come back from work and we feel fatigued and exhausted, and if a child is noisy or demanding our attention and we cannot provide it, then we might use corporal punishment.

It is therefore not merely about changing a behaviour, but also about releasing your anger and your stresses. These are the things that we as adults and parents need to learn — to be alerted to our own emotions, to our way of coping with difficult stresses from our colleagues, our bosses or from other areas in our lives. So, instead of beautifying or justifying a certain way of disciplining our children, go more in depth and try to find out what is in the best interests of your child and even for yourself. If we want to set boundaries and limits with our children, I think we have to first start with ourselves.

We have to look around and reflect on what the good practices are, and what the essence of adopting such practices is. Why do we not allow other people to hit us so easily, even when we're not doing things to meet their needs? Say, for example, between spouses — why are we saying that domestic violence should be prohibited? Why is it that domestic violence should not be sanctioned? Why is it that there should be no violence in a couple's relationship? If this is the case, then let us try our very best to use other, more effective non-violent means to parent our children as well.

To trace trends, characteristics and root causes, Hong Kong piloted an Advisory Review Panel, which presented two reports, and formed an ongoing Child Fatality Review Panel, which presented four more reports. Yet the system, not addressing specific death cases and being advisory, shoulders no monitoring role.

Some fundamental systems are still outstanding and need to be addressed. A child fatality inquiry and a mandatory reporting system would ensure that serious cases are identified and help is brought in promptly. A comprehensive child law reform to reflect the UNCRC stipulations is essential. While the government has started consultations on mandatory reporting, there are hesitations. First, there is concern about the possibility of a sudden increase in caseload and whether the existing manpower would be able to cope. Second, the definition of serious harm is non-specific. Third, there is concern about punishing professionals in the frontline and adversely affecting their relationship with clients. Fourth, families may be reluctant to seek help because of the law. All of these must be thoroughly addressed. However, a firm emphasis on children's best interests and well-being must be the way forward.

Question: What is the role of schools in managing suspected cases of abuse, and how can schools safeguard the well-being of children?

Answer: Apart from when they are at home, our children spend a lot of time in school. Therefore school personnel need to understand that their role goes beyond just teaching the curriculum. We have a common goal that is in the UNCRC, that the child has a right to survive. If some of the children are not surviving well or are at risk, even if we teach they wouldn't be able to learn well.

If we ask ourselves what is in the best interests of children, it is really their safety and whether they are in a condition to actually learn. The main thing that we have in our education system is the ability to facilitate, to empower and to strengthen the resilience, curiosity and initiative of our children. This will enable them to live out their potential and develop into responsible and dignified persons. This should be the foremost mission of our education system.

If we find any children too tired or always hiding themselves in a corner during recess, teaching or designated professionals should go forward and try to understand them better. In that sense, the school can do something and, as I mentioned, every school needs a safeguarding policy that is widely disseminated. Every member under the school's umbrella should be aware of their duties, not only with their own tasks but also with overriding core responsibilities that everyone in the same school has to shoulder. That being said, if we wish for our school personnel to do a decent, satisfying and caring job, I think we need to put in place training and support at all levels.

With schools, one more area is parents' involvement. It's important to work with the parents. This tripartite partnership of parents, teachers and children is important. Our system needs to ensure that personnel and resources are in place in order for parents to come into the picture because eventually children will be going home and will be under their parents' care. We are not there to see some of the things children experience at home; these are not made visible to us. We wouldn't know, so we have to work together with their parents too.

Positive Parenting and Community Empowerment

For a caring and non-violent childhood, the law alone is not enough. Building a caring, respecting and violence-free culture must be made a norm.

A violence-free notion must start at home. Positive parenting in the family, starting from early childhood, matters. Community empowerment paves the way for a hopeful future. The values of self-discipline, responsibility, respect, public good and consideration for the rights of others — children and adults — form the important cornerstones of parenting. Let me share two evidence-based effective programmes for your consideration.

Head Start Home Visitation Programme

In one of the international conferences, the Head Start programme was shared and inspired the operations in Hong Kong, leading to ACA rendering a modified version, sustained through the decades by experienced and dedicated volunteers who were caring mothers themselves. They were first trained and then helped to train and support others in marching through a challenging new start for their families.

The Hong Kong government, inspired by the concept, specified the importance of the 0 to 5 early childhood years in its policy address and devoted resources to start off a comprehensive Child Development Service in 2005. The project, which has been sustained up to the present, involves a collaboration between the Hong Kong Department of Health's Hospital Authority, the Social Welfare Department, the Education Bureau and NGOs.

In view of resource constraints, instead of making the project universal, four types of at-risk groups are chosen as targets:

1. At-risk pregnant women
2. Mothers with postnatal depression

3. Children and families with psycho-social needs

4. Pre-primary children with physical, developmental and behavioural needs

However, it is important to set up support networks and to build and strengthen family resilience before problems surface. Child advocates have been calling for a review of this 16-year-old programme, to trace trends and characteristics, assess impact, understand programme value and expand the scope of support and empowerment to more children and families in Hong Kong.

Triple P — Positive Parenting Programme

Another evidence-based programme worth mentioning is the Triple P — Positive Parenting Programme for families with children aged 0 to 16 years in Australia. The programme gives parents the tools to take their stress out and encourage positive behaviour from children by dealing positively and consistently with problem behaviours and developing intimate positive family relationships. Triple P offers practical skills and tools to help parents:

*   Develop positive relationships with their child

*   Set family routines and rules that work

*   Manage problem behaviour and support positive behaviour

*   Raise well-adjusted, emotionally resilient children

*   Balance work and family with less stress

*   Create a happier, safer, more supportive family so they can be the parents they want to be

The Queensland government has invested over AUD12 million to implement a state-wide roll out of Triple P and to provide the programme free-of-charge to all parents of children below the age of 16. To date, in Queensland alone, over 210,000 parents have participated in Triple P.

Question: Would compulsory stage-based parenting training be productive in raising relationally and emotionally healthier children, and in preventing abuse?

Answer: I think parent support, parent education and parent training are lifelong. Being a parent really involves a lifetime commitment of supporting our family and children. Having said that, it doesn't mean that we encourage dependency. Our child management or child-rearing pendulum shouldn't swing to the two extremes, from the extreme of using harsh punishment to the other extreme of indulgence.

People are concerned that this pendulum is swinging to one side, such that children are the kings or tyrants in their families. That is problematic and not what we want to see. If that is the case, we have to put our foot down and ask ourselves what kind of children, what kind of parenting, in principle, we want to see as a community consensus?

With parenting, the ideal is for every parent to be properly supported and educated. As the saying goes, the seeds have been sown and the trees will be grown. Let's not wait until the last moment when you're bearing the baby that you're doing something. Of course, when you're actually having a baby there's much to learn. There is the Head Start programme I mentioned earlier, which is very effective and evidence-based. The support comes in right from when the child is born because this is a very critical moment. The programme involves actually going to your home and helping you to identify what are safe and unsafe kinds of furniture or arrangements, as well as how to ensure the child is properly cared for. Providing all these to a parent with a newborn and at the same time allowing the parent to share, to ventilate stresses and concerns, helps a great deal. It helps to reduce postpartum depression after the delivery.

Of course, there are other difficulties and demands as the child grows up. Therefore, parent education should start early and follow through different stages for parents to actually learn and not just be given a model to copy. There's no model for all, but there are overarching parenting principles, guidelines and directions that we can all hopefully turn to.

Child Empowerment and Participation

A truly shared journey safeguarding our future must include our children. Children are stakeholders and they not only have things to say but also have much to offer. They are the potential change agents.

Make our reconstruction map child-friendly and empower children to participate.

The UNCRC stipulates, in Article 12(1), "State Parties shall assure to the child who is capable of forming his or her own views, the right to express those views freely in all matters affecting the child, the views of the child being given due weight in accordance with the age and maturity of the child."

And Article 13(1) indicates that "The child shall have the right to freedom of expression; this right shall include freedom to seek, to receive and impart information and ideas of all kinds, regardless of frontiers, either orally, in writing or in print, in the form of art, or through any other media of the child's choice."

Article 13(2) must also be emphasised and be included in child rights education. It indicates that "The exercise of this right may be subject to certain restrictions, but these shall only be such as are provided by law and are necessary."

a.   For respect of the rights or reputation of others; or

b.   For the protection of national security or of public order, or of public health or morals

But to ensure constructive participation, the child must be fully informed, in their own language, in a child-friendly setting, at their own pace and, if necessary, to be separately represented. They must also be promised confidentiality in what they share, for their case to be promptly handled and for their views to be given due weight. These are principles which adults must learn to acquire.

Through the decades, Hong Kong has been trying to honour the commitment of respecting child participation by first piloting and then implementing various ongoing child participation pro- grammes. To name a few:

Let the Dolphin Lead is a programme ACA started, based on the notion that children are endangered in different ways, just as what our lovely dolphins have been experiencing in the Hong Kong waters because of natural and man-made pollution. We had invited children from higher forms to join and receive train- ing as mentors to lead and guide children in lower forms, through music, play, artwork, surveys and debates — for their articulations on family, school, the community and the government. Their works and their voices were shared in a large-scale public forum and presented to key government officials and the Chair of the Youth Commission.

The programme has evolved into a Children's Council to repli- cate the Legislative Council System in Hong Kong, with children as councillors who make their own selection of topics for their research and conduct interviews with key opinion leaders in the public and private fields. At the beginning stage, the project attracted only elite schools which sent their students, but along the way all types of schools had students joining and actively participating. The Hong Kong Legislative Council had, in the past, let us use their chamber for the programme. Currently, we have transferred to the university chambers for our meeting venues; we express our special appreciation to the Hong Kong Constitutional and Mainland Bureau for funding the project through the years.

There are government-led child participation programmes in Hong Kong as well. The Hong Kong Legislative Council hearings have for quite some years included children for verbal and written submissions in their hearings of important issues impacting children. The government has also set up a Children's Forum for child representatives and child advocates. Child engagement programmes have been organised, particularly for children with specific needs.

Overseas countries' experiences of child participation started early. Norway started as early as 1981 with considering children as expert advisors. Their ombudsman has been regularly meeting with children and listening to their voices. New Zealand's Prime Minister Jacinda Ardern had, during the pandemic, met children online to understand their needs. Scottish cabinet meetings have been receiving members of their Children's Parliament to understand their concerns. One of the very impressive experiences has been that of the Australian Children's Commissioner's *Big Banter* national listening tour to hear the views of children and their advocates throughout Australia. The commissioner had met face to face with over 1,000 children and online with another 1,400 children, as well as with child advocates to explore issues most important to children. The five most mentioned areas by children and advocates were as follows:

1. A right to be heard

2. Freedom from violence, abuse and neglect

3. The opportunity to thrive

4. Engaged citizenship

5. Action and accountability of policymakers and authorities

There are also inspiring surveys and studies that convey children's voices and their inner workings. We as adults must help children to build capacity, increase resilience, equip them with skills, knowledge and opportunities to harness their energy for positive change and to face the ever-changing world. We have to believe that children and youths have the potential to create solutions for the unique challenges of their generation.

The WHO is right to say that no one is safe until everyone is safe. For everyone to be safe, we must come together to rebuild our world. Though the pandemic has exerted such a strong, destructive force upon us, a pandemic solidarity is still possible in bringing the best out of people, reminding us that acts of kindness, such as supporting each other, volunteering for each other, singing to one another and sharing and donating to others, have remained so important in helping to counter threats and desperation.

We salute our selfless medics and healthcare personnel who have taken risks and made great sacrifices in order to keep us safe. Let these beautiful acts lift our spirits up. To spread love and not hatred. And to remind us that there is no quarantine on kindness.

Let children be our shared vision, our common goal and purpose of the journey in reconstructing a future that is welcoming, safe, caring and respectful for us all. Show children how to respect the rights of others, by us demonstrating respect for their rights.

The Book Committee

The Book Committee was responsible for interviewing the speakers for their post-lecture reflections, sourcing images and illustrations, weaving the six lectures into a single book and overseeing the publication process.

Tan Seok Hui (Chair) — Chairperson, Research Committee, Singapore Children's Society. She is also the Vice-Chairperson of the Research and Advocacy Standing Committee and a member of the Board.

Lin Xiaoling — Director, Research and Advocacy Department, Singapore Children's Society. She has been a staff member since 2010.

Grace Yap — Assistant Manager, Research and Advocacy Department, Singapore Children's Society. She worked for the Society from 2013 to 2019 and rejoined as a staff member in 2021.

www.ingramcontent.com/pod-product-compliance
Lightning Source LLC
Chambersburg PA
CBHW071745270326
41928CB00013B/2802